The FAMILY IMMUNITY COOKBOOK

The FAMILY IMMUNITY COOKBOOK

101 EASY RECIPES TO BOOST HEALTH

TOBY AMIDOR

Robert ROSE

Library and Archives Canada Cataloguing in Publication
Title: The family immunity cookbook : 101 easy recipes to boost health / Toby Amidor.
Names: Amidor, Toby, author.
Description: Includes index.
Identifiers: Canadiana 2021017983X | ISBN 9780778806806 (softcover)
Subjects: LCSH: Cooking (Natural foods) | LCSH: Functional foods. | LCSH: Immunity—Nutritional aspects. | LCSH: Nutrition. | LCGFT: Cookbooks.
Classification: LCC TX741 .A45 2021 | DDC 641.5/63—dc23

Disclaimer
The recipes in this book have been carefully tested by our kitchen and our tasters. To the best of our knowledge, they are safe and nutritious for ordinary use and users. For those people with food or other allergies, or who have special food requirements or health issues, please read the suggested contents of each recipe carefully and determine whether or not they may create a problem for you. All recipes are used at the risk of the consumer.

We cannot be responsible for any hazards, loss or damage that may occur as a result of any recipe use.

For those with special needs, allergies, requirements or health problems, in the event of any doubt, please contact your medical adviser prior to the use of any recipe.

At the time of publication, all URLs referenced link to existing websites. Robert Rose Inc. is not responsible for maintaining, and does not endorse the content of, any website or content not created by Robert Rose Inc.

DESIGN AND PRODUCTION: Kevin Cockburn/PageWave Graphics Inc.
PHOTOGRAPHY, FOOD STYLING AND PROP STYLING: Ashley Lima
EDITOR: Kate Bolen
PROOFREADER: Mikayla Butchart
INDEXER: Ken Della Penta
CONCRETE TEXTURE: © gettyimages.com

Published by Robert Rose Inc.
120 Eglinton Avenue East, Suite 800, Toronto, Ontario, Canada M4P 1E2
Tel: (416) 322-6552 Fax: (416) 322-6936
www.robertrose.ca

Printed and bound in China

1 2 3 4 5 6 7 8 9 LEO 29 28 27 26 25 24 23 22 21

to Micah, Ellena and Schoen —

Usually I dedicate my books to you in age order,

but to be fair, this time I reversed it.

I love you all very much.

CONTENTS

INTRODUCTION

Worrying about your family's wellness is stressful.

As a busy working mom with three kids, keeping my family healthy is a priority, and I know how overwhelming it can be to figure out the best way to do that. Fortunately we have help. Our bodies have a built-in defense against illness: the immune system.

A healthy immune system is vital to good health. The immune system helps fight off any foreign invaders to the body. If our immune systems are healthy, it's easier to fight bacteria, viruses or anything else trying to make us sick. A global pandemic has shaken the way we view our health and that of our families, and it's easy to feel like the odds are stacked against us. Research has even started to reveal that unhealthy eating can potentially impair the immune system's response to vaccines, including COVID-19. Keeping your family's immune systems strong and resilient is your first-line defense for safeguarding their health. It is more important now than at any other point in our lives to make sure our immune systems are operating at peak efficiency.

But that sounds complicated. How do we build healthy immune systems anyway? Simple. As a dietician, it's my job to know how to keep our bodies strong and working to the best of their ability, and it all starts with what you eat. A healthy diet keeps your immune system in optimum shape. If you have a subpar diet, improving what you eat can also help improve your immunity. Unfortunately, during times of high stress, it's easy to forget how much we benefit from eating well.

To make healthy eating a little easier, in chapter 1, I break down the concept of eating well so it's easy to understand and do. Our bodies get different nutrients from different foods, so when we do not eat a balanced and varied diet inclusive of fruits, vegetables, proteins, starches (including whole grains), milk and dairy products, and healthy fats, we can miss out on some (or even many) of the things that keep our immune systems healthy and working properly. In chapter 2, I identify twenty-five of the top immune-boosting foods and incorporate them into the 101 recipes in this book. These are ingredients that provide immune-essential nutrients to keep your body's defenses in tip-top shape, or they are foods that help decrease inflammation and boost antioxidant activity, which helps your body defend itself from illness and can also promote healing. Adding these twenty-five foods to your family's well-balanced diet is an important part of maintaining and helping enhance their healthy immune systems.

When you combine healthy eating with staying hydrated, getting plenty of sleep, exercising regularly, consuming alcohol in moderation and finding good ways to deal with stress, you set up your family's immune systems to be at their best—and hopefully set up to be sick less often or prepare their bodies to fight off an illness when they do get sick. In the pages ahead I've included guidance on how to help your family do just that, as well as tips and tricks for getting healthy, well-balanced meals on the table with less stress.

With my own children, I tried very hard to develop their healthy eating habits early on. If these habits are established in childhood, and sustained throughout adulthood, the impact on health can be profound. We all want lifelong wellness for our families, so let's set them up for success. Starting now.

*Wishing you and your family
happy, healthy cooking!*

HEALTHY HABITS TO STRENGTHEN YOUR IMMUNE SYSTEM

Your body has a network of tissues, cells and organs that tries to keep out foreign invaders such as bacteria and viruses. This is your immune system. Some of the main parts of the immune system include white blood cells, antibodies and the lymphatic system. All of these parts, and others, actively fight foreign bodies that enter your body.

The main goal of this cookbook is to keep your immune system in tip-top shape so if a foreign invader attacks, your body is ready. This means living the healthiest lifestyle possible, which includes the six habits described below. In addition to the six habits, this chapter guides you through establishing a healthy eating plan, helps you build an immune-boosting day and provides tips for minimizing stress in the kitchen. At the end of the chapter you'll find a quick self-assessment to gauge how well your lifestyle is currently supporting your immune system.

6 Habits to Energize Your Immune System

1 | KEEPING HYDRATED

Approximately 60% of your body is made of water. Keeping hydrated is important for your overall health because water plays an essential role in keeping your body's systems working efficiently—including your immune system. Mild dehydration doesn't lead to illness, but it can wreak havoc on your body, causing headaches, dizziness or digestive problems. It can also affect your mood, memory and how well you are able to process information. Once you are properly hydrated, these milder symptoms go away. To prevent dehydration, drink plenty of fluids daily. Water is the top fluid recommendation because it doesn't contain calories. Seltzer, sparkling water and calorie-free flavored seltzers or waters are also good choices. Other beverages that count toward hydration include 100% fruit juice and milk. If you choose to drink juice, choose 100% fruit or vegetable juice, and keep portions at $^1/_2$ cup (125 mL) to 1 cup (250 mL) since juices do contain calories. If you drink milk, opt for low or nonfat milk whenever possible to help minimize calories, added sugar and saturated fat. Coffee and tea also count toward hydration, but minimize the amount of sugar and cream you add, and avoid prepackaged sweetened coffee and tea beverages to help minimize the calories and saturated fat you are consuming. Sweetened drinks such as sodas, lemonade and sports drinks certainly help you stay hydrated, but they should be minimally consumed because of the added sugar. Fruits and vegetables also contribute to fluid needs, which is one reason it's so important to eat plenty of them.

2 | GETTING PLENTY OF SLEEP

Not getting enough shut-eye has been linked to poor dietary choices, increased risk of chronic diseases like heart disease and type 2 diabetes, reduced psychological well-being and a decreased lifespan. There is scientific evidence that not getting enough sleep can reduce the capabilities of the body's immune system.[1] Some research shows that a lack of sleep can result in an increase in white blood cells, which indicates inflammation.[2] It can also make you more susceptible to getting sick if you're exposed to a disease-causing microorganisms and cause illness recovery to take longer.[3] Overall, getting plenty of sleep allows your immune system to stay healthy and better fight off illness. Adults should aim to get at least 7 hours of sleep every night, teenagers need 8 to 10 hours every night and younger children and infants should get up to 14 hours (including naps).

> A few tips to help you sleep better include limiting screen time at least an hour before bed, sleeping in a dark room or using a sleep mask, keeping a sleep schedule and going to bed the same time nightly and exercising regularly.

3 | EXERCISING REGULARLY

Regular physical activity helps strengthen your immune system. Moderate physical activity may help reduce inflammation and help immune cells regenerate regularly. Moderate exercise includes activities such as jogging, swimming, bicycling, playing tennis doubles, heavy cleaning (such as vacuuming and mopping) and mowing the lawn. Choose activities that you enjoy doing or exercise with a friend. Aim for at least 150 minutes of moderate physical activity every week. It's always a good idea to speak with your physician before beginning an exercise program.

1 Luciana Besedovsky, Tanja Lange and Jan Born, "Sleep and Immune Function." *Pflugers Archiv: European Journal of Physiology* 463, no. 1 (November 2012): 121-37, https://doi.org/10.1007/s00424-011-1044-0.

2 Karim Zouaoui Boudjeltia, Brice Faraut, Patricia Stenuit, Maria José Esposito, Michal Dyzma, Dany Brohée, Jean Ducobu, Michel Vanhaeverbeek and Myriam Kerkhofs, "Sleep Restriction Increases White Blood Cells, Mainly Neutrophil Count, in Young Healthy Men: A Pilot Study," *Vascular Health and Risk Management* 4, no. 6 (2008): 1467-70, https://doi.org/10.2147/vhrm.s3934.

3 "NIOSH Training for Nurses on Shift Work and Long Work Hours: Sleep and the Immune System," The National Institute for Occupational Safety and Health (NIOSH), Centers for Disease Control and Prevention, last reviewed March 31, 2020, https://www.cdc.gov/niosh/work-hour-training-for-nurses/longhours/mod2/05.html.

4 | CONSUMING ALCOHOL IN MODERATION

Drinking too much alcohol can compromise your immune system, making it harder for it to defend your body against foreign invaders. In addition, alcohol can trigger inflammation in the gut and have a negative impact on the good bacteria living there that keep your immune system healthy.

> If you choose to drink alcohol, it's important to drink in moderation, which is defined as no more than 1 drink per day for a woman and 2 drinks per day for a man. One drink is defined as 12 fl oz (375 mL) of regular beer, 5 fl oz (150 mL) of wine or 1½ fl oz (45 mL) of 80 proof liquor like rum or vodka. Unfortunately, you can't "save" your drinks for Saturday night. This is the maximum consumption per day.

5 | HEALTHY EATING

A healthy diet is an important part of building a healthy immune system. Although there is no one food that will magically make your immune system perfect, including a variety of immune-boosting foods that play various roles in building and maintaining your immune system can certainly help. In the following sections you will find guidelines on a healthy eating plan (page 17) and how to build an immune-boosting day (page 22). In chapter 2, you will find a description of twenty-five foods to include in your diet that, together with a healthy eating plan, can help boost your immune system. Throughout this cookbook you will find recipes from breakfast to snacks to soups to main meals that include one or more of the immune-boosting foods in them.

Each recipe in this book lists the number of immune-boosting ingredients it contains.

6 | FINDING GOOD WAYS TO DEAL WITH STRESS

Scientific evidence suggests that there is a mind-body interaction, and being stressed can weaken the body's ability to fight infection. Fortunately, when we find good ways to deal with stress, such as exercise, meditation, yoga or talking to a friend, it helps our bodies stay healthier. You can also look for ways to minimize stress. When it comes to healthy cooking and eating, tactics like meal prepping, freezing foods, cooking one-pot meals and cooking meals that take 30 minutes or less from start to finish are great ways to make things less stressful in the kitchen. See page 23 for more on that topic.

What Is a Healthy Eating Plan?

A healthy eating plan is one that contains a variety of foods including fruits, vegetables, starches, protein, milk and dairy foods and healthy fats. These foods ideally should be consumed in three meals with between one and three snacks a day. Spacing out the meals throughout the day allows enough time for the nutrients in the meal or snack to be properly absorbed. Part of an immune-boosting diet is making sure to take in a variety of foods, so your body gets the nutrients you need to keep it in tip-top shape.

> Spacing meals throughout the day allows enough time for the nutrients to be properly absorbed.

FRUITS AND VEGETABLES

According to the Centers for Disease Control (CDC), one in ten individuals meet the recommended daily amount for fruits and vegetables. Fruits and vegetables provide fiber, vitamins, minerals and phytonutrients, which are natural plant compounds that help keep you healthy and help prevent disease. There are numerous phytonutrients that also have been shown to help keep your immune system healthy. They are found in many of the twenty-five immune-boosting foods listed in chapter 2.

STARCHES

Starches are a form of carbohydrates that the body uses for energy. When choosing starches, you want at least half to come from whole grains. Whole grains foods include whole wheat pasta, 100% whole wheat bread, quinoa, brown rice, farro, oats, barley, bulgur and millet. Whole grains provide fiber and numerous vitamins and minerals. Fiber provides many health benefits, such as keeping your gastrointestinal tract healthy, helping lower cholesterol levels, helping control blood sugar levels and even helping with weight loss because it makes you feel full for longer. In addition, research now suggests that the health of your digestive system directly impacts immunity, and a healthy digestive system can help reduce inflammation in the body. Although oats are a whole grain listed in the twenty-five immune-boosting foods, all forms of whole grains should certainly be part of a healthy immune-boosting diet. Starchy vegetables like potatoes, sweet potatoes and corn are also part of this group and provide a variety of important vitamins and minerals along with fiber.

PROTEIN

Protein foods can be from animal foods, like eggs, chicken, beef, pork or lamb, or from plant-based foods, like beans, lentils, tofu and nuts. When choosing animal-based proteins, opt for lean or extra-lean choices or remove the skin from poultry and trim visible fat from meats before eating to minimize the amount of saturated fat you are consuming. It's important to keep an eye on portions of animal-based proteins like poultry and meat, which should be about 3 to 4 oz (90 to 125 g) cooked. Lean animal proteins contribute a variety of important nutrients to the diet including iron, zinc and numerous B-vitamins. Plant-based proteins also contribute nutrients such as iron, fiber, vitamin E and healthy fats. Both animal-based and plant-based proteins can be part of a healthy eating plan and both provide numerous immune-boosting nutrients.

> Both animal-based and plant-based proteins can be part of a healthy eating plan.

MILK AND DAIRY FOODS

Milk and other dairy are another group of foods that contribute numerous nutrients such as calcium, vitamin D, potassium, phosphorus, magnesium, vitamin B_{12} and zinc. This group also includes foods like Greek yogurt, traditional yogurt, kefir, cottage cheese, ricotta cheese, Cheddar and many other cheeses. Opt for nonfat or low-fat dairy whenever possible to help minimize how much saturated fat you are consuming. If you're lactose intolerant, many lactose-free milk and dairy products can be found in grocery stores. You can also opt for soy milk and soy yogurt, which is the closest plant-based beverage nutrition-wise compared to cow's milk.

HEALTHY FATS

Monounsaturated and polyunsaturated fats are considered healthy fats, and they are important to incorporate into your diet. They have numerous functions in your body, such as carrying fat-soluble vitamins A, D, E and K through your bloodstream and keeping you satisfied after eating a meal because they take longer to digest. You can find healthy fats in a variety of foods like avocado, olives and oils like canola, olive, peanut, sunflower and avocado oils. Healthy fats can also be found in nuts and nut butters, as well as in seed and seed butters (like sunflower seed butter).

FILLING YOUR PLATE

It's easier than you think to get well-balanced meals on the table when you consider how to fill your plate. Take a 9-inch (23 cm) plate and imagine it in three parts: one half and two quarters. When creating your meals, fill half your plate with fruits and vegetables. Next fill one-quarter of your plate with starches, preferably whole grains. Fill the last quarter of your plate with lean protein, from plants or animals.

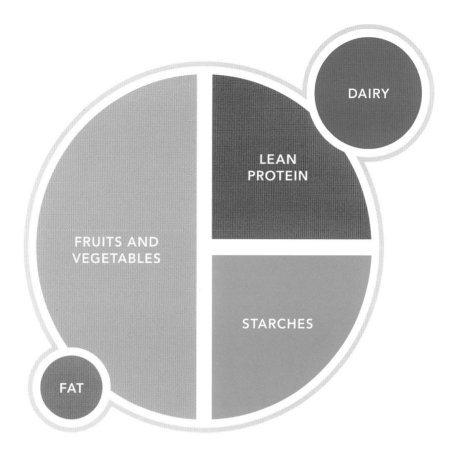

Also, include a small amount of healthy fat: add a slice of avocado to your plate, use a healthy oil (like olive or canola) to cook the meal or dress a salad with a vinaigrette. And don't forget to add dairy like a glass of milk, or shredded cheese over your pasta or rice. Eating a variety of foods enables you to take in a variety of nutrients that your body needs to stay healthy.

When you prepare and eat snacks, think of them as mini meals, which should consist of healthy foods. If you find yourself hungry between meals, especially if you go about 5 hours between them, then it's a good time to insert a snack. Include two or three food groups in your snacks. The more variety, the more good-for-you nutrients you'll take in. Try to include at least some form of healthy fats, fiber or protein because those three nutrients help keep you feeling full for longer. For example, dip pears in peanut butter or top nonfat plain Greek yogurt with almonds and strawberries.

TOP 25 IMMUNE-BOOSTING FOODS

1. GARLIC
2. YOGURT
3. BEEF
4. LENTILS
5. SUNFLOWER SEEDS
6. EGGS
7. RED BELL PEPPERS
8. ALMONDS
9. ORANGES
10. STRAWBERRIES
11. GINGER
12. GRAPES
13. SPINACH
14. MUSHROOMS
15. SWEET POTATOES
16. ASPARAGUS
17. CHICKPEAS
18. SALMON
19. TURMERIC
20. WALNUTS
21. OATS
22. AVOCADOS
23. GREEN TEA
24. PEARS
25. CAULIFLOWER

How to Build an Immune-Boosting Day

In chapter 2 you will find details about twenty-five immune-boosting foods that you can incorporate into your healthy eating plan. Give your immune system an extra boost by including at least five of these immune-boosting foods in your diet every day. Meals and snacks both count toward your total five (or more), so there are plenty of opportunities throughout the day to take them in.

Below you'll find a sample immune-boosting day using the recipes in this cookbook. Each recipe provides you with the number of immune-boosting foods it contains. The more immune-boosting foods you can include every single day, the better!

	BREAKFAST	SNACK 1	LUNCH	SNACK 2	DINNER
	Green Tea Smoothie Bowl with Raspberries (page 55)	Pear with 1 tbsp (15 mL) almond butter	Smashed Chickpea and Sunflower Sandwich (page 129) with 2 clementine oranges	Spiced Cauliflower "Popcorn" (page 109) with 1 hard-cooked egg	Branzino with Tomato, Olive and Garlic Sauce (page 182); brown rice and a tossed salad with lettuce, tomatoes, cucumbers and red bell peppers, topped with 2 tbsp (60 mL) vinaigrette
Immune-Boosting Foods	3	2	3	3	3

How to Minimize Stress in the Kitchen

When life is feeling stressful, the task of getting food on the table can feel like another hurdle. In this section you'll find four ways to help minimize the daily stress of feeding your family, which include meal prepping, creating freezer-friendly foods, cooking one-pot meals and finding healthy recipes that take 30 minutes or less from start to finish.

Look for these icons throughout the book to quickly see the time-saving and dietary features of each recipe. Some recipes are easily adapted to different diets. See Toby's Tips for ideas.

ONE-POT
Can be made in one pot or pan, or in a blender (for smoothies).

30 MINUTES OR LESS
Takes 30 minutes or less to make, from start to finish.

MEAL PREP
Make in advance and eat it all week long.

FREEZER-FRIENDLY
Finished dish freezes well.

VEGETARIAN
Does not contain meat, poultry or seafood.

VEGAN
Does not contain any animal products.

DAIRY-FREE
Does not contain milk or dairy products (like cheese and yogurt).

GLUTEN-FREE
Does not contain wheat or gluten.

MEAL PREPPING

Take the stress out of mealtime by choosing a day or two prepare foods for the entire week. Below are the five steps to take when meal prepping.

STEP 1: CHOOSE WHEN TO MEAL PREP

Setting aside time on Sundays to meal prep for the week ahead often works well, but you can also choose to split it over two days. Estimate 4 or 5 hours of prep work and cooking, which should help shave off at least an hour from the actual time you spend on the day you are serving it.

STEP 2: DECIDE WHICH MEALS TO PREP

A few days before you meal prep, plan your meals. Start by deciding how many recipes you will be making. If you're not used to meal prepping, then build your way up. For example, the first week, only meal prep two different dinners. The following week you can meal prep one breakfast and two different dinners.

Meals should also be well-balanced with vegetables, fruits, starches, lean protein, dairy and healthy fats. Also, read through each of the recipes to determine that the ingredients are easy to find and that you have all the equipment needed to make the recipe. Check that the recipe takes a reasonable amount of time to prep and cook and that it's simple to prepare. If you or people in your family have any food allergies or specific health concerns, reading through the recipe can help identify if it meets the needs of your family.

STEP 3: GO FOOD SHOPPING

The day before you meal prep, buy your groceries. Gather your recipes before heading to the market. Read through each one and write a shopping list. Check your refrigerator, freezer and pantry to avoid buying duplicate ingredients and help minimize food waste and unnecessary expense. Write your shopping list according to the flow of the supermarket, saving refrigerated and frozen items for the end.

Don't forget to bring your own grocery bags.

Set aside one to two hours for grocery shopping. Don't forget to bring your own grocery bags. Be sure to minimize the time the food spends in your car, especially on a hot day. Use a cooler and ice, if needed, and make the shopping trip the last stop before you head home.

STEP 4: PREP AND COOK

Before you begin cooking, prep ingredients for all of your recipes that require an extra step, such as washing and chopping all of the fruits and vegetables or chopping nuts. Prepare the ingredients for the recipes that take the longest to cook first so you can get those dishes started.

Next, before you start cooking, make sauces and dressings, including marinades, dressings and bread crumbs. Then, start by cooking longer recipes first, like Chickpea Stew (page 172). While the dish is cooking, prep other ingredients or complete a couple of quick and easy recipes. Shorter recipes, such as a dip or a snack, can be prepared during down time while another recipe is cooking. Finally, make the remaining recipes. Most, if not all, of the ingredients should already be prepped, so those last few recipes should be a breeze.

STEP 5: PORTION AND PACK

To ensure that you have enough food for everyone, it's important to portion and pack. Before placing the food in the refrigerator or freezer, label it with the name of the dish and how long it will last. Extra servings can be frozen and saved for another busy week.

FREEZER-FRIENDLY FOODS

Cook a double batch of a recipe and freeze one for a later date. You can choose to freeze the family-size batch or in individual portions. Recipes like pastas, soups and meats with sauces are good to freeze. Salads and sandwiches typically are not good for freezing. To freeze, place the food into a freezer-friendly container or sealable plastic bag. Label it with the name of the dish and the use-by date two months from freezing. To thaw, refrigerate overnight. After thawing, reheat it in the oven, on the stove or in the microwave in a covered microwave-safe dish, until an instant-read thermometer inserted into the thickest part registers 165°F (74°C).

ONE-POT MEALS

Save time in the kitchen with one-pot and sheet pan meals. Sheet Pan Salmon with Asparagus (page 174) is an example of a one-pan meal that's cooked in 30 minutes or less, with salmon and asparagus cooked at the same time on a single baking sheet. Many soups, including Hearty Lentil-Tomato Soup (page 118), also use one pot, which helps minimize dishes. Both one-pot and sheet pan dinners are stress-reducers when you have to get dinner on the table in a flash.

30 MINUTES OR LESS

When you can complete a recipe from start to finish within 30 minutes or less it's a total win! One shortcut to help get a meal on the table is to use canned or frozen foods. For example, instead of soaking and cooking beans, purchase low-sodium canned beans. Taking these shortcuts helps shave off minutes to hours in the kitchen. Examples of recipes that take 30 minutes or less include Tropical Oatmeal (page 60), Almond Butter and Pear Toast (page 65), Immune-Boosting Green Tea Smoothie (page 79), Walnut Date Energy Bites (page 104) and Salmon BLT (page 132).

QUIZ How Strong Do You Keep Your Immune System?

This quiz can help you assess if your daily habits are supporting your immune system or if yours is in need of a little (or big) boost! For each question, choose the response that best reflects your personal habits.

1 **Realistically, I sleep:**
A Barely enough, maybe 4 hours a night if I'm lucky.
B I think I'm okay with 5 to 6 hours a night.
C Like a baby. I sleep 7 to 8 hours a night or more.

2 **I describe my stress levels as:**
A High: When can I go on vacation?
B Medium: Every now and then I let it get to me.
C Low: I am super chill.

3 **In a week, I like to drink alcohol:**
A Four or more times a week, and I often have a second or third round.
B Two or three times a week, socially or with dinner.
C Maybe once a week with dinner.

4 **I typically exercise:**
A Does walking to my car and back count? Maybe 30 minutes a week.
B If it's not too busy of a week, I'll squeeze one or two workouts in! About 45 to 60 minutes each.
C Working out is part of my daily routine. I definitely get in at least 150 minutes of moderate activity every week.

5 **I eat walnuts, almonds or sunflower seeds:**
A If I remember where I put them in my pantry, a couple times a month.
B Once or twice a week.
C At least a handful four or more times a week!

6 **I like to include oatmeal or yogurt in my meals:**
A Almost never (0 to 1 times per week).
B Sometimes (2 to 3 times per week).
C Almost daily (4 or more times per week).

7 **I include chickpeas, asparagus or cauliflower in my meals:**
A Almost never (0 to 1 times per week).
B Sometimes (2 to 3 times per week).
C Almost daily (4 or more times per week).

8 | I include spinach, red bell peppers or sweet potatoes in my meals:
A Almost never (0 to 1 times per week).
B Sometimes (2 to 3 times per week).
C Almost daily (4 or more times per week).

9 | I include oranges, strawberries, grapes or pears in my weekly meals:
A Almost never (0 to 1 times per week).
B Sometimes (2 to 3 times per week).
C Almost daily (4 or more times per week).

10 | I include garlic, ginger, turmeric and green tea in my meals:
A Almost never (0 to 1 times per week).
B Sometimes (2 to 3 times per week).
C Almost daily (4 or more times per week).

11 | I include salmon, eggs, mushrooms and avocado in my meals:
A Almost never (0 to 1 times per week).
B Sometimes (2 to 3 times per week).
C Almost daily (4 or more times per week).

12 | I include beef or lentils in my weekly meals:
A Almost never (0 to 1 times per week).
B Sometimes (2 to 3 times per week).
C Almost daily (4 or more times per week).

SCORING

Add up your score. For each A add 0 points, for each B add 1 point and for each C add 2 points. Total your points and read below to see how well you maintain your immune system.

0 TO 8 POINTS: You have some work to do. Poor habits such as little sleep and exercise, paired with high stress and alcohol consumption can be detrimental to your immune system. The foods included in this quiz (and detailed in chapter 2) provide a multitude of vitamins and minerals that are important to keep your immune system healthy. Continue reading to learn manageable ways to incorporate these foods and habits into your daily life.

9 TO 16 POINTS: You're getting there, but your immune system still could use a boost! Keep reading for additional tips and recipes for how to better support your immune system.

17 TO 24 POINTS: Excellent work! You're already practicing a healthy lifestyle and eating habits to support your immune system. The important part now is to keep it up! The recipes in this cookbook can help add variety and new recipes to your immune-boosting lifestyle.

25 FOODS TO BUILD YOUR IMMUNE SYSTEM

The following twenty-five foods provide nutrients to keep your immune system healthy. For each food, you will find a description of its immune-boosting properties, shopping tips, storage tips and recipes in this cookbook that use it. I recommend incorporating at least five of these foods into your family's meals and snacks every day.

1 GARLIC

WHY THIS FOOD?

Provides antioxidants and sulfuric compounds. Recent research has shown that garlic stimulates a variety of cells linked to the immune system.

Garlic provides small amounts of important vitamins and minerals, such as the antioxidant vitamin C, vitamin B_6, selenium and potassium. In addition, garlic contains over one hundred sulfuric compounds, which research suggests provides the anti-inflammatory properties in garlic. A 2015 review[1] of recent research concluded that garlic appears to boost the immune system's functions by stimulating cells linked to the immune system. As an added bonus, one clove of this aromatic vegetable provides only four calories.

SHOPPING TIP: Choose unblemished garlic bulbs that are tight and firm with dry skin.

STORAGE TIP: Store garlic in an open or ventilated container in a cool, dark place for up to 3 months. Once the bulb has been separated into cloves, use within about 10 days.

RECIPES WITH GARLIC

- Spinach and Mushroom Egg Bake p. 61
- Garlic Dip p. 95
- Garlic and White Bean–Stuffed Mushroom Caps p. 169
- Garlic Shrimp with Chickpeas p. 177
- Branzino with Tomato, Olive and Garlic Sauce p. 182
- Creamy Farro with Garlic and Spinach p. 214
- Garlic Soy Mushrooms p. 220

2 YOGURT

WHY THIS FOOD?

Provides live, active cultures that may act as probiotics, which can help boost the immune system.

Whether you choose traditional or Greek yogurt, this fermented dairy product contains live, active cultures. These probiotics act as "good" bacteria in your digestive system, which means they provide health benefits and help protect the digestive tract. Research has shown that some strains of probiotics can help boost your immune system and promote a healthy digestive system.

---

1 Rodrigo Arreola, Saray Quintero-Fabián, Rocío Ivette López-Roa, Enrique Octavio Flores-Gutiérrez, Juan Pablo Reyes-Grajeda, Lucrecia Carrera-Quintanar and Daniel Ortuño-Sahagún, "Immunomodulation and Anti-Inflammatory Effects of Garlic Compounds," *Journal of Immunology Research*, vol. 2015, Article ID 401630, 13 pages, 2015. https://doi.org/10.1155/2015/401630.

SHOPPING TIP: Look for "live, active cultures." If you don't see the term "live, active cultures" on the container, check the ingredients list for the names of bacteria like *L. acidophilus* and *L. thermophiles*, which indicate they are present.

Do not leave yogurt at room temperature for over 2 hours.

STORAGE TIP: When you buy yogurt, be sure to refrigerate it immediately after arriving home. Store it in the coldest part of your refrigerator, toward the back and away from the door. The shelf life of yogurt is 7 to 14 days. To use, spoon the portion of yogurt needed from a larger size container and place the remaining yogurt back in the refrigerator. Do not leave yogurt at room temperature for over 2 hours. If it's over 90°F (30°C), then do not leave it out for over 1 hour.

RECIPES WITH YOGURT

- Green Tea Smoothie Bowl with Raspberries p. 55
- Poached Pear Yogurt Bowl p. 59
- Orange Greek Yogurt Pancakes with Strawberry Sauce p. 70
- Immune-Boosting Green Tea Smoothie p. 79
- Pear Ginger Smoothie p. 82
- Yogurt "Caramel" Dip with Pears p. 96
- Strawberry Kiwi Almond Yogurt Bark p. 99
- Herbed Turkey Chickpea Meatballs with Yogurt Sauce p. 186
- Yogurt Marinated Pork Kebabs p. 206
- Greek Yogurt Chocolate Mousse with Strawberries p. 234
- Grape Popsicles p. 243

3 BEEF

WHY THIS FOOD?

Top source of zinc, which can help rev up your immune system defenses.

Zinc is a mineral involved in many metabolic activities in your body, including the production of protein and wound healing. It also plays a role in immune function. Because the body doesn't store zinc, it is important to get zinc daily, and one of the best sources is beef. On average, a 3 oz (90 g) cooked serving of beef provides 39% of the recommended daily value of zinc. To maintain a healthy diet, choose lean cuts of beef whenever possible.

SHOPPING TIP: Packages of beef will specify the cut, weight, price per pound, total price, sell-by date and safe handling instructions.

Purchase your beef on or before the sell-by date. Look for beef that is bright, cherry red and firm to the touch. If the beef is in a vacuum-sealed bag, the color is typically darker purplish-red. Once it's exposed to the air, it will turn that bright, cherry red color. Make sure the package is cold and has no holes or tears. Choose packages without excess liquid. For ground beef, you'll see the percent lean to percent fat. For example, you'll see "90% lean; 10% fat."

STORAGE TIP: When shopping for beef, place it in your cart just before checkout. If it takes more than an hour to drive home, consider keeping the beef in a cooler in your car. Once home, refrigerate or freeze immediately. Freeze beef in its original packaging for up to 2 weeks. If you plan to store it longer, wrap it in heavy-duty aluminum foil or place it in sealable plastic freezer bags, removing as much air as possible. When storing beef in your refrigerator, place it on the lowest shelf on a plate or tray to catch any juices. Label each package in your refrigerator or freezer with the date, name of beef cut and weight or number of servings. Use refrigerated beef roasts or steaks within about 3 days of purchase. Ground beef should be used within 1 to 2 days of purchase.

> Ground beef should be used within 1 to 2 days of purchase.

RECIPES WITH BEEF
- Vegetable Beef Soup p. 122
- Roast Beef and Sautéed Onion Sandwich p. 139
- Balsamic Steak Salad p. 157
- Beef and Rice–Stuffed Peppers p. 197
- Beef and Mushroom Bolognese with Penne p. 198
- Steak Pizza with Peppers and Onions p. 201
- Beef and Sweet Potato Bowls p. 202

4 LENTILS

WHY THIS FOOD?

Good plant-based source of zinc and vitamin B_6, both of which play a role in your immune system's defense.

Lentils are a good plant-based source of zinc, with 1 cup (250 mL) of cooked lentils providing 17% of the recommended daily dose of the mineral. This legume is also an excellent source of iron, providing 37% of the recommended daily amount, and a good source of vitamin B_6, providing 18% of the recommended daily amount. Zinc, iron and vitamin B_6 all help create infection-fighting white blood cells.

SHOPPING TIP: At the market, look for dried lentils near the packaged beans and rice. They may also be found in the soup aisle. Choose packages that do not contain holes and are clean and sealed. Canned lentils can be found next to the canned beans. Choose cans that are not leaking, bulging, dented, rusted or without a label.

STORAGE TIP: Store dried or canned lentils in the pantry in a cool, dry place. Dried lentils can be stored for up to 1 year from the date of purchase and after opening. Canned lentils can be stored unopened for 2 to 5 years. Once opened, transfer the contents to a sealable container and store in the refrigerator for up to 5 days.

RECIPES WITH LENTILS
- Lentil-Stuffed Eggplant p. 162
- Lentil Shepherd's Pie p. 165
- Hearty Lentil-Tomato Soup p. 118
- Jasmine Rice with Peas and Lentils p. 216

5 SUNFLOWER SEEDS

WHY THIS FOOD?

Provides vitamin E, selenium, copper and manganese, all needed to maintain — and even boost — your immune system.

Just 1 oz (28 g) of sunflower seeds is an excellent source of the antioxidant vitamin E, selenium, copper and manganese. Vitamin E is essential for the body and it helps boost the immune system so it can fight off invading bacteria and viruses. Selenium plays a critical role in protecting the body from chronic inflammation and infection. Copper and manganese are minerals that both help maintain your immune system.

RECIPES WITH SUNFLOWER SEEDS
- Nut and Seed Breakfast Cookies p. 69
- Nut and Seed Clusters p. 100
- Carrot Sunflower Mini Muffins p. 106
- Smashed Chickpea and Sunflower Sandwich p. 129

SHOPPING TIP: Sunflower seeds are stocked near the nuts and are available salted or unsalted and in shell or shelled. For the recipes in this book, look for shelled raw or unsalted dry roasted sunflower seeds. Look for clean and sealed packages, without any rips or holes.

STORAGE TIP: Store unopened bags or containers of sunflower seeds in your pantry in a cool, dry place away from the sunlight. After opening, store the seeds in an airtight container in a cool, dark location in your pantry for up to 4 months.

6 | EGGS

WHY THIS FOOD?

Provides vitamins D and E, critical for a healthy immune system.

One large egg provides thirteen vitamins and minerals and high-quality protein, all for 70 calories. The egg white certainly contains protein, but that golden yolk also provides a boatload of these important nutrients. Vitamin D, found in the yolk, is critical for your immune system to function properly and for bone health. Eggs are one of the only foods that naturally contain this important vitamin. Vitamin E is also found in the yolk and is involved in immune function.

SHOPPING TIP: Check for clean, uncracked shells that are stored in a refrigerated case. Do not buy eggs that are past their "use by" or "sell by" date. Choose the most useful and economical egg size. The recipes in this cookbook call for large eggs. The color of the shell doesn't matter because it isn't related to quality. Rather, the shell indicates the color of the chicken's ear lobes. (Yes! Chickens have ear lobes.)

STORAGE TIP: Store eggs in the coldest part of the refrigerator and never in the refrigerator door. Store them in their original package for up to 5 weeks in the refrigerator or for up to 1 year in the freezer. If an egg cracks in the carton, break it into a clean bowl or container, cover tightly and place in the refrigerator for up to 2 days.

> Store eggs in the coldest part of the refrigerator and never in the refrigerator door.

RECIPES WITH EGGS

- Spinach and Mushroom Egg Bake p. 61
- Breakfast Quesadilla with Egg, Spinach, Red Pepper and Bacon p. 62
- Berry-Stuffed French Toast p. 73
- Egg-Stuffed Bell Peppers with Tomato and Mozzarella p. 107
- Avocado Egg Salad–Stuffed Pita p. 136
- Barbecue Chicken Cobb p. 158

7 | RED BELL PEPPERS

WHY THIS FOOD?

Excellent source of the antioxidant vitamin C, which plays a role in immune function.

Just $^1/_2$ cup (125 g) cup of sweet red bell pepper provides over 100% of the daily recommended amount of vitamin C. In addition to its function as an antioxidant, several cells of the immune system need vitamin C to perform their task. In addition, research shows that vitamin C may slightly reduce the duration of an illness in a healthy person.[2] Red bell peppers provide the antioxidant vitamins A and E, which also help fight free radicals that can damage your body's cells.

SHOPPING TIP: Choose peppers that are firm, bright, shiny and heavy for their size. Avoid peppers with bruises and soft spots, or those that are shriveled or soft.

STORAGE TIP: Store peppers in a plastic bag in the refrigerator for up to 1 week.

RECIPES WITH RED PEPPERS

- Breakfast Quesadilla with Egg, Spinach, Red Pepper and Bacon p. 62
- Egg-Stuffed Bell Peppers with Tomato and Mozzarella p. 107
- Orzo Salad with Red Bell Peppers and Mozzarella p. 149
- Cilantro-Lime Salad with Grilled Chicken and Avocado p. 154
- Whole Roasted Cauliflower with Tomato-Pepper Ragu p. 170
- Chicken Stir-Fry with Red Peppers, Broccoli and Walnuts p. 194
- Beef and Rice–Stuffed Peppers p. 197
- Steak Pizza with Peppers and Onions p. 201
- Roasted Bell Pepper and Mozzarella Couscous p. 213

8 ALMONDS

WHY THIS FOOD?

Brimming with the antioxidant vitamin E, which helps keep your immune system healthy.

—

Just 1 oz (30 g), or 23 almonds, of unsalted dry roasted almonds provides 169 calories, 6 grams of plant protein, 3 grams of fiber, "good" unsaturated fats, magnesium and vitamin E. The antioxidant vitamin E is fat-soluble and found in high concentrations in immune

---

2 Alexander Ströhle and Andreas Hahn, "Vitamin C und Immunfunktion [Vitamin C and immune function]," *Med Monatsschr Pharm*, 32, no.2 (Feb 2009):49–54; quiz 55-6, German, https: //pubmed.ncbi.nlm.nih.gov/19263912.

cells compared to other cells in the blood. It's one of the most effective nutrients that helps keep your immune system working properly.[3] Plus almonds add a delicious crunch to dishes.

SHOPPING TIP: Almonds are available shelled and unshelled and with and without salt. Look for almonds in the baking or snack aisle or the produce section of the market. Slivered, sliced and chopped almonds should be white throughout. Avoid those that are rancid and yellow in color. For in-shell almonds, the nuts should not rattle when you shake them, which would indicate they are old.

STORAGE TIP: Unopened packages of shelled almonds can be stored in the refrigerator or pantry for up to 2 years. Once opened, store in a cool, dry place in an airtight container for up to 3 months.

RECIPES WITH ALMONDS

- Poached Pear Yogurt Bowl p. 59
- Almond Butter and Pear Toast p. 65
- Nut and Seed Breakfast Cookies p. 69
- Pear-Ginger Smoothie p. 82
- Strawberry Kiwi Almond Yogurt Bark p. 99
- Nut and Seed Clusters p. 100
- Spinach Salad with Strawberries and Almonds p. 142
- Soba Noodle Salad with Almond-Ginger Dressing p. 150
- Almond Crusted Snapper p. 173
- Quinoa and Almond Pilaf p. 211

 # ORANGES

WHY THIS FOOD?

Plethora of vitamin C in both the flesh and zest helps the immune system work properly.

One medium orange provides 78% the recommended daily amount of vitamin C. This antioxidant vitamin can increase the production of white blood cells, which help fight infection. Vitamin C also helps absorb the mineral iron from plant sources (like spinach and black beans) and helps the immune system work properly to help protect the body from disease. The zest (or peel) of an orange also provides vitamin C, plus, it adds great flavor to recipes! Other citrus fruits like lemons, limes, grapefruit and more also provide vitamin C and should certainly be included in an immune-boosting diet.

---

3 Erin Diane Lewis, Simin Nikbin Meydani and Dayong Wu, "Regulatory role of vitamin E in the immune system and inflammation," *IUBMB Life* 71, no. 4 (April 2019): 487–494, https://doi .org/10.1002/iub.1976.

Citrus fruits like lemons, limes, grapefruit and more also provide vitamin C and should certainly be included in an immune-boosting diet.

SHOPPING TIP: Look for oranges that are heavy for their size and bright in color. They should be firm and smooth without mold or bruises.

STORAGE TIP: Store oranges at room temperature for 1 to 2 days. They can also be stored in the refrigerator for up to 2 weeks.

RECIPES WITH ORANGES

- Orange Greek Yogurt Pancakes with Strawberry Sauce p. 70
- Whole Wheat Cranberry-Orange Loaf p. 74
- Citrus Spritzer p. 89
- Chicken Breasts with Orange-Fig Sauce p. 193
- Orange Poached Pears p. 236

10 STRAWBERRIES

WHY THIS FOOD?

Provide numerous antioxidants, including vitamin C and ellagic acid, which play a role in immune function.

One serving of 8 strawberries — equivalent to 1 cup (250 mL) — provides the recommended amount of vitamin C needed for an entire day. Vitamin C plays a role in immune function, and also helps form essential parts of your body like blood vessels, muscles and collagen in bones. These red-hued berries also provide ellagic acid, a phytochemical naturally found in strawberries that has antioxidant properties.

SHOPPING TIP: Choose strawberries that are bright red in color with a natural shine and fresh-looking green caps.

STORAGE TIP: Store strawberries in the refrigerator for up to 7 days. Keep dry while storing and don't wash until just before serving.

RECIPES WITH STRAWBERRIES

- Orange Greek Yogurt Pancakes with Strawberry Sauce p. 70
- Berry-Stuffed French Toast p. 73
- Strawberry-Oat Smoothie p. 85
- Strawberry Limeade p. 90
- Strawberry Kiwi Almond Yogurt Bark p. 99
- Strawberry Avocado Toast p. 110
- Spinach Salad with Strawberries and Almonds p. 142
- Cod with Strawberry Salsa p. 178
- Greek Yogurt Chocolate Mousse with Strawberries p. 234
- Fresh Strawberry Cupcakes with Strawberry Glaze p. 240

11 | GINGER

WHY THIS FOOD?

Contains a variety of powerful antioxidants that may help reduce inflammation.

The ginger that we commonly eat is the root of the ginger plant. It has a peppery flavor with a slight sweetness and a pungent, spicy aroma. Ginger contains a variety of powerful antioxidants including gingerols, shogaols and zingerones that may help reduce inflammation. In addition, initial research has shown that ginger may be beneficial for combating bacterial infections.[4]

SHOPPING TIP: Ginger comes is a variety of forms including fresh, ground, dried, pickled and crystallized. The recipes in this cookbook call for either fresh or ground. Fresh ginger can be found in the produce aisle at the market. Look for fresh ginger with shiny skin that is not thick and fibrous. You should be able to easily scratch the skin with your nail. Ground ginger can be found in the spice aisle at the market. Dried ground ginger is much stronger than the fresh, so be careful when substituting it in a recipe.

STORAGE TIP: Store fresh ginger tightly wrapped in plastic for up to 3 weeks in your refrigerator or up to 6 months in your freezer. Store dried ginger in a cool, dry place for up to 2 years.

RECIPES WITH GINGER
- Poached Pear Yogurt Bowl p. 59
- Pear Ginger Smoothie p. 82
- Roasted Spiced Chickpeas p. 103
- Ginger Chicken Soup p. 125
- Soba Noodle Salad with Almond-Ginger Dressing p. 150
- Gingerbread Chia Pudding p. 237

> Look for fresh ginger with shiny skin that is not thick and fibrous.

12 | GRAPES

WHY THIS FOOD?

Contain numerous antioxidants and polyphenols that protect the body's cells, as well as resveratrol, which helps with healthy immune function.

---

4 Arshad H. Rahmani, Fahad M. Al Shabrmi and Salah M. Aly, "Active ingredients of ginger as potential candidates in the prevention and treatment of diseases via modulation of biological activities." *International Journal of Physiology, Pathophysiology and Pharmacology* 6, no. 2 (July 2014): 125–36. https://www.ncbi.nlm.nih.gov/pmc/articles/PMC4106649.

One of the most critical components to immune health is proper hydration. Grapes are 82% water and can help keep you hydrated. They contain over 1,600 plant compounds that may help fight and prevent disease. Some of the compounds in grapes include antioxidants and polyphenols, which protect the health and function of the body's cells. Grapes also contain resveratrol, which helps regulate immunity and helps fight inflammation. Resveratrol may also play a beneficial role in the prevention and progression of chronic diseases related to inflammation including diabetes, obesity, cardiovascular disease and cancers.[5]

SHOPPING TIP: Grapes come in a variety of colors including black, green, and red. Look for grape bunches with green, pliable stems and plump berries. The powdery-white coating on grapes is called bloom, which protects grapes from moisture loss and decay (so it's good!).

To avoid odor absorption, do not store grapes next to onions or leeks.

STORAGE TIP: Store grapes in the refrigerator unwashed and dry for up to two weeks and rinse before serving. To avoid odor absorption, do not store grapes next to onions or leeks.

RECIPES WITH GRAPES
- Grape Oatmeal Cups p. 56
- Grape Slushie p. 83
- Skillet Chicken with Rosemary and Grapes p. 190
- Roasted Brussels Sprouts with Grapes p. 228
- Grape Popsicles p. 243

13 SPINACH

WHY THIS FOOD?

Includes numerous antioxidants and iron — all of which are involved in keeping your immune system healthy.

All antioxidants are involved in the immune system. They help fight free radicals that can cause damage to your cells, and spinach provides antioxidant vitamins A, C and E. In addition to those and other numerous nutrients found in spinach, it is also a source of iron. It's important to note that iron is an under-consumed nutrient by most people around the world, and iron deficiency anemia can impair your

[5] Lucia Malaguarnera, "Influence of Resveratrol on the Immune Response," *Nutrients* 11, no. 5 (April 2019): 946, https://doi.org/10.3390/nu11050946.

immune function. When consuming iron from a plant source, like spinach, pair it with a source of vitamin C (like orange juice or oranges) to aid iron absorption.

SHOPPING TIP: Spinach is available fresh, frozen and canned. Many of the recipes in this cookbook call for fresh baby spinach, which is often found in convenient pre-washed ready-to-eat packages in the produce section of your market. Choose spinach that is crisp and bright green with no signs of insect damage or discoloration of the leaves.

STORAGE TIP: Store fresh spinach bunches loosely wrapped in a damp paper towel and wash thoroughly immediately before preparing. Prepackaged baby spinach should be stored in its original packaging. Both fresh spinach bunches and packaged baby spinach should be stored in the refrigerator and used within 3 to 5 days.

RECIPES WITH SPINACH

- Spinach and Mushroom Egg Bake p. 61
- Breakfast Quesadilla with Egg, Spinach, Red Pepper and Bacon p. 62
- Green Tea Smoothie Bowl with Raspberries p. 55
- Immune-Boosting Green Tea Smoothie p. 79
- Chicken, Mushroom and Avocado Quesadilla p. 189
- Grilled Portobello Mushroom Caprese Sandwich p. 135
- Spinach Salad with Strawberries and Almonds p. 142
- Pasta with Chicken, Spinach and Mushrooms p. 185
- Brown Rice with Spinach and Mushrooms p. 210
- Creamy Farro with Garlic and Spinach p. 214
- Sautéed Spinach with Fennel and Red Onion p. 223

 14 # MUSHROOMS

WHY THIS FOOD?

Brimming with nutrients that keep your immune system functioning properly, including copper, zinc and L-ergothioneine.

There are many varieties of mushrooms, including the three called for in recipes in this cookbook: white button (referred to in these recipes simply as "mushrooms"), cremini (sometimes labeled as baby bella) and portobello. Mushrooms, especially the brown varieties, are an excellent source of copper, providing 22% of the daily recommended amount per 1 cup (250 mL) of whole mushrooms. Copper is involved in many metabolic processes in the body, including your immune system functioning. If you don't get enough copper, it can result in compromised immune function and possibly increase the incidence of infection. Zinc is another nutrient found in mushrooms that also plays a role in a healthy immune system. A deficiency in zinc, even mild or moderate, can compromise the immune system and impair the body's defense cells. In addition, mushrooms contain a powerful antioxidant called L-ergothioneine, which also helps regulate the immune system.

SHOPPING TIP: Choose fresh mushrooms that are firm and evenly colored. Avoid those that are broken, damaged or have soft spots. If all the gills are showing, the mushroom is no longer fresh.

STORAGE TIP: Store unwashed mushrooms in the refrigerator in a paper bag for 5 to 6 days.

RECIPES WITH MUSHROOMS

- Spinach and Mushroom Egg Bake p. 61
- Chicken, Mushroom and Avocado Quesadilla p. 189
- Grilled Portobello Mushroom Caprese Sandwich p. 135
- Barbecue Chicken Cobb p. 158
- Garlic and White Bean–Stuffed Mushroom p. 169
- Halibut Marsala p. 181
- Pasta with Chicken, Spinach and Mushrooms p. 185
- Beef and Mushroom Bolognese with Penne p. 198
- Brown Rice with Spinach and Mushrooms p. 210

15 SWEET POTATOES

WHY THIS FOOD?

An excellent source of beta-carotene.

The orange-colored flesh of this sweet root vegetable is an excellent source of beta-carotene, which is converted to vitamin A in the body. Vitamin A helps fight inflammation and plays a critical role in enhancing the immune function. The vitamin is involved in the development of the immune system and in regulating how immune cells respond in the body. Low blood levels of the vitamin have been linked to reduced immunity.

SHOPPING TIP: Select sweet potatoes that are firm with intact skin and no large dents or blemishes.

STORAGE TIP: Store in a cool, dry place for up to 4 weeks.

RECIPES WITH SWEET POTATOES

- Lentil Shepherd's Pie p. 165
- Sweet Potato Rounds Topped with Goat Cheese, Pecans and Cranberries p. 114
- Spiced Sweet Potato Soup p. 128
- Roasted Sweet Potato Salad with Avocado p. 146
- Sweet Potato Mash p. 224

16 ASPARAGUS

WHY THIS FOOD?

Provides a plethora of nutrients that help with immune function, including antioxidant vitamins A and C, iron and copper.

Asparagus is filled with the immune-boosting nutrients iron, copper and antioxidant vitamins A and C. Both vitamins A and C help fight free radicals that damage cells, and vitamin C helps build the immune system. Iron is the most common vitamin or mineral deficiency in the world, and a lack of this mineral can lead to impaired immune function. Copper is also involved in proper immune system function, and raw asparagus provides 28% of the recommended daily amount per 1 cup (250 mL). If you don't get enough copper, it may increase the incidence of infection.

SHOPPING TIP: Choose asparagus bunches that are straight, firm and bright in color. The spears should be of a similar thickness so they cook evenly. The feathery tips should be tightly closed.

STORAGE TIP: Store asparagus in a plastic bag or upright in a container with a little water and place in the refrigerator for up to 3 days.

RECIPES WITH ASPARAGUS

- Creamy Asparagus Soup p. 121
- Sheet Pan Salmon with Asparagus p. 174
- Turkey and Asparagus Penne p. 196
- Steamed Asparagus with Lemon Butter p. 219

17 CHICKPEAS

WHY THIS FOOD?

Contain numerous nutrients that build your immune system, including vitamin B_6, vitamin C, iron, zinc and copper.

Nutrients in chickpeas that help build up your immune system include vitamin B_6, the antioxidant vitamin C, iron, zinc and copper. Vitamin B_6 is heavily involved in immune function. For example it helps promote production of components of the immune system called lymphocytes, which are white blood cells that are also one of the body's main types of immune cells. Iron, the most common deficiency in the world, is important to get enough of. If you become iron deficient, it can impair how well your immune system works. Zinc helps fight infections and heal wounds, while copper is required by the immune system to perform several important functions.

SHOPPING TIP: Chickpeas, also known as garbanzo beans, can be found dried or canned. At the market, look for canned chickpeas in the bean aisle or ethnic food section. Choose cans that do not have dents, leaks or bulging lids. The recipes in this cookbook use canned chickpeas; however, cooked dried chickpeas can be used instead.

STORAGE TIP: Store dried chickpeas in a cool, dry place and use within 1 year. Canned chickpeas should be stored in a cool, dry place and be used between 2 and 5 years from the date of purchase. Once opened, transfer the chickpeas to a sealable container and store in the refrigerator for up to 4 days.

RECIPES WITH CHICKPEAS

- Roasted Turmeric Ginger Chickpeas p. 103
- Smashed Chickpea and Sunflower Sandwich p. 129
- Chickpea and White Bean Burgers p. 166
- Chickpea Stew p. 172
- Garlic Shrimp with Chickpeas p. 177
- Herbed Turkey Chickpea Meatballs with Yogurt Sauce p. 186
- Immune-Boosting Brownies p. 248

18 SALMON

WHY THIS FOOD?

A wonderful source of omega-3 fats, which have anti-inflammatory properties.

Fatty fish, including salmon, contain a healthy amount of the omega-3 fats EPA and DHA. Omega-3s are a type of polyunsaturated fatty acid (PUFA). There are three major types of omega-3s including alpha-linolenic acid (ALA), eicosapentaenoic acid (EPA) and docosahexaenoic acid (DHA). ALA comes from plants and is a true "essential" omega-3 because we need to get this fat from the diet, as our bodies cannot make it on their own. ALA is found in seeds like flax and chia, nuts like walnuts and oils like soybean and canola. ALA can be converted to EPA and DHA in the body, but the process is not very efficient. EPA and DHA are fatty acids found naturally in marine sources, and the most common food source of both are fatty fish. EPA and DHA have been shown to be the most protective of the heart. Evidence also supports the role of EPA and DHA for prenatal development, specifically for brain and eye health. Both EPA and DHA are found in all cells of the body and also have been shown to have anti-inflammatory functions, which could potentially increase the body's ability to fight off illness.

SHOPPING TIP: For this cookbook the recipes use fresh salmon, but you can also use frozen and thawed salmon. When purchasing fresh salmon, it should smell like fresh fish with no fishy odor, and the flesh should spring back to the touch. Frozen salmon should not have large ice crystals, which could mean it was defrosted and then refrozen (a sign that it may be spoiled).

Fresh salmon should smell like fresh fish with no fishy odor.

STORAGE TIP: Store fresh salmon in the refrigerator at 41°F (5°C) or below for up to 2 days. To freeze fresh salmon, wrap the fish tightly in a layer of plastic wrap followed by a layer of aluminum foil and then freeze for up to 3 months. If the salmon is already frozen from the store, freeze in original packaging for up to 3 months.

RECIPES WITH SALMON
- Smoked Salmon Crostini p. 113
- Salmon BLT p. 132
- Chopped Salad with Salmon p. 152
- Sheet Pan Salmon with Asparagus p. 174

19 TURMERIC

WHY THIS FOOD?

Contains curcumin, which is thought to help stimulate the immune system.

The potent antioxidant properties thought to be found in curcumin help protect cells and fight inflammation. In addition, some initial research suggests that both turmeric and its component curcumin may help stimulate the immune system.

SHOPPING TIP: The recipes in this cookbook use ground turmeric, although it is available as turmeric root as well. Ground turmeric can be found in the spice aisle at the market.

STORAGE TIP: Store ground turmeric in a cool, dry place for 2 to 3 years in your pantry after opening.

RECIPES WITH TURMERIC
- Pineapple-Turmeric Smoothie p. 80
- Golden Milk p. 86
- Roasted Spiced Chickpeas p. 103
- Spiced Cauliflower "Popcorn" p. 109
- Spiced Sweet Potato Soup p. 128
- Golden Cauliflower Salad p. 153
- Golden Pork Chops p. 205

WALNUTS

WHY THIS FOOD?

Brimming with omega-3 ALA, vitamin B$_6$ and polyphenols that can help your immune system.

This tree nut is an excellent source of omega-3 ALA (alphalinolenic acid) and a good source of vitamin B$_6$, both of which are part of a functioning immune system. Walnuts also have the highest amount of the natural plant compound called polyphenols compared to other tree nuts and peanuts, which may play a role in supporting heart health and cognitive health. It also helps fight inflammation and combat some diseases like cancer. In addition, good gut health has been linked to numerous health benefits for digestion, metabolism and the immune system. Walnuts have been shown to have prebiotic properties, that have been shown to be a good choice for gut health.

SHOPPING TIP: You can find walnuts in-shell or shelled. The recipes in this cookbook used shelled walnuts that are raw or unsalted and dry roasted. You can also find walnuts sold as halves, halves and pieces, pieces or chopped. Shelled walnuts are available in bags and bulk bins. Look for them in the produce section, as well as in the snacking and baking aisles at your market.

Shelled walnuts are available in bags and bulk bins.

STORAGE TIP: If you plan to use them immediately, the best place to store walnuts is in your refrigerator. Walnuts become rancid when exposed to warm temperatures for a long period of time. The heat causes the fat in the walnuts to have off odors and flavors. They should have a mildly nutty aroma and sweet taste. Rancid walnuts smell like paint thinner and should be thrown out. If you are going to be storing them for at least a month, then store them in your freezer in a sealable plastic bag.

RECIPES WITH WALNUTS

- Chocolate Chip Walnut Muffins p. 66
- Nut and Seed Breakfast Cookies p. 69
- Nut and Seed Clusters p. 100
- Walnut Date Energy Bites p. 104
- Pear Salad with Walnuts and Dried Cranberries p. 145
- Chickpea and White Bean Burgers p. 166
- Chicken Stir-Fry with Red Peppers, Broccoli and Walnuts p. 194
- Chocolate-Dipped Walnuts p. 233
- Banana Walnut Cake with Cream Cheese Frosting p. 244

21 OATS

WHY THIS FOOD?

Provide beta-glucan, selenium, zinc, arginine and the natural plant compound avenanthramides, all of which help boost immune function.

Beta-glucan is a type of fiber found in oats that helps boost white blood cells, which that help fight infection. The minerals selenium and zinc also help fight off infection and keep your immune system healthy. In addition, beta-glucan can help trigger a series of chemical activities in the body that help the immune system function more efficiently. Oats are also brimming with the amino acid arginine that helps heal injuries, regulate blood flow and boost the immune system. Selenium is a mineral that also helps regulate the immune response and acts as an antioxidant protecting your cells from oxidative damage and infection. Oats also provide a natural plant compound called avenanthramides, which has antioxidant properties and can potentially minimize inflammatory responses and stimulate the immune system.

SHOPPING TIP: There are a variety of oats available at the market. The recipes in this cookbook use large flake (old-fashioned) rolled oats, which means the oats have been steamed and flattened with a roller into large, thick flakes. Quick-cooking rolled oats are rolled thinner and require a shorter cooking time compared to large flake (old-fashioned) rolled oats. Steel-cut oats (also known as Irish or Scottish oats) are processed by chopping the whole oat groat into several pieces, rather than rolling them. Steel cut oats take the longest to cook, and they have a chewy texture. The oats retain most of their shape even after cooking. You can find oats in the cereal or breakfast aisle in your market or in bulk bins.

STORAGE TIP: Store oats tightly sealed in the original container in a cool, dry place for up to 4 months or in the freezer in a sealable bag for up to 8 months from the date of purchase.

RECIPES WITH OATS
- Grape Oatmeal Cups p. 56
- Tropical Oatmeal p. 60
- Nut and Seed Breakfast Cookies p. 69
- Strawberry-Oat Smoothie p. 85
- Chocolate Oat Cookies p. 239

22 AVOCADOS

WHY THIS FOOD?

Provide numerous nutrients to help your immune system, including unsaturated fat, vitamin E, vitamin B$_6$, copper and zinc.

Avocados contain unsaturated fat, which acts as an immune system nutrient booster because it helps transport fat-soluble vitamins A, D, E and K through the body. In addition, avocados provide the antioxidant vitamin E, which helps keep the immune system strong against potentially harmful microorganisms like viruses and bacteria. Vitamin B$_6$ helps the body create antibodies that are produced by the body when it detects foreign invaders like viruses and bacteria. Avocados also provide the minerals copper and zinc, both of which help keep your immune system healthy.

SHOPPING TIP: Avocados are a fruit that ripen off the tree, which is why you often find them unripe at the market. When shopping, look for avocados that feel heavy for their size. If you are buying Hass avocados, those commonly found in grocery stores, the skin should be dark, with a little green and no dents or bruises.

STORAGE TIP: If you bought an unripe Hass avocado that is hard to the touch, green and unripe, put it in a brown paper bag out of the sunlight for 3 days. To speed up the ripening process, add an apple or banana to the bag along with the avocado. The ethylene gas produced by apples and bananas will help speed up the ripening process. A ripe avocado is slightly tender to the touch but not overly soft. To store avocados after cutting, squeeze a little lemon or orange juice or it and wrap tightly in plastic wrap. Store in the refrigerator for 1 to 2 days.

> A ripe avocado is slightly tender to the touch but not overly soft.

RECIPES WITH AVOCADOS

- Strawberry Avocado Toast p. 110
- Chicken, Mushroom and Avocado Quesadilla p. 189
- Chipotle Chicken Sandwich with Avocado p. 131
- Avocado Egg Salad–Stuffed Pita p. 136
- Roasted Sweet Potato Salad with Avocado p. 146
- Cilantro-Lime Salad with Grilled Chicken and Avocado p. 154
- Barbecue Chicken Cobb p. 158

23 GREEN TEA

WHY THIS FOOD?

Contains powerful antioxidants called polyphenols that fight disease, as well as antioxidant vitamins C and E.

—

Green tea contains a plethora of polyphenols, powerful antioxidants shown to help fight disease. Polyphenols tend to activate signaling of different pathways in the immune system when a foreign invader is present to help the body respond in whatever way is necessary to help fight it. That bitter flavor you taste in over-steeped green tea is from one of the catechins (a specific type of polyphenol, or natural plant compound). That is why you'll see instructions in this cookbook to steep your green tea for exactly 3 minutes to avoid that bitterness. Other immune-boosting nutrients found in green tea include the antioxidant vitamins C and E.

SHOPPING TIP: The recipes in this cookbook call for green tea bags. You can find packages of tea bags in the coffee and tea aisle at your grocery store. Loose leaf green tea is also available. If your local market doesn't carry it, check with your local specialty food store.

STORAGE TIP: Store the package of tea in a cool, dry place for 8 to 36 months from the date of purchase. Once opened, the tea bags should be used within 6 to 12 months. Loose tea leaves can be stored in the pantry for 2 years from the date of purchase and 6 to 12 months after opening.

RECIPES WITH GREEN TEA

- Green Tea Smoothie Bowl with Raspberries p. 55
- Immune-Boosting Green Tea Smoothie p. 79

- Skillet Green Tea Vegetables p. 227

PEARS

WHY THIS FOOD?

Flavonoids and vitamin C provide antioxidant functions to possibly help fight infection.

Pears provide flavonoids, which are antioxidants that help fight inflammation, lower the risk for infection, possibly lower the risk of disease and improve immune function. In addition, pears are a good source of the antioxidant vitamin C. Pears are also an excellent source of fiber, providing over 20% of the recommended daily amount. A 2013 review found that fiber may play a role in regulating the immune system and fighting inflammation. It may also help decrease the risk of inflammation-related conditions, such as cardiovascular disease, cancer, obesity and type 2 diabetes.[6]

SHOPPING TIP: Choose firm pears with the stem intact. Pears don't ripen on the tree. They ripen from the inside out at room temperature. To check if a pear is ripe, "check the neck" by applying gentle pressure to the stem end (or "neck") of the pear. If it yields to pressure, then it is ripe and ready to enjoy.

Choose firm pears with the stem intact.

STORAGE TIP: Once the pear is ripe, it can be placed in the refrigerator to slow the ripening process and be used within 5 days. If you bought an underripe pear, store it in a bowl near other ripening fruit like bananas, which naturally produce a gas called ethylene that helps speed the ripening process.

---

6 Joanne Slavin, "Fiber and prebiotics: mechanisms and health benefits." *Nutrients* 5, no. 4 (April 2013): 1417-35, https://doi.org/10.3390/nu5041417.

25 CAULIFLOWER

WHY THIS FOOD?

Provides numerous immune-boosting nutrients including vitamin C, vitamin B_6 and natural plant compounds called carotenoids and flavonoids.

The immune-boosting goodness in cauliflower comes from vitamins C and B_6 and from phytonutrients, which are natural plant compounds that help keep you healthy and protect or fight against disease, called carotenoids and flavonoids. The antioxidant vitamin C is known to help fight inflammation and boost immune health. Vitamin B_6 helps create infection-fighting white blood cells. Both carotenoids and flavonoids are natural compounds found in cauliflower that have antioxidant properties to help fight disease and protect oxidative damage on cells.

SHOPPING TIP: When selecting fresh cauliflower, choose a head that feels firm, heavy, and compact. The color of the head should be creamy white and the leaves should be fresh and not wilted. You may also find orange, green, and purple cauliflower when they're in season, so feel free to swap them in for the traditional white variety.

STORAGE TIP: Store whole cauliflower unwashed in loosely sealed plastic in your refrigerator for up to 10 days. Wash before eating.

CHAPTER 3

BREAKFASTS

Green Tea Smoothie Bowl
WITH RASPBERRIES

SERVES 2

SERVING SIZE
1 bowl

IMMUNE-
BOOSTING
FOODS: ③

Raspberries are another food that will help your body's defense system. One cup of fresh raspberries provides an excellent source of the antioxidant vitamin C, which plays an important role in the immune system. These juicy morsels also provide anthocyanins, which are powerful antioxidants that help fight inflammation and regulate immune responses.

Blender

1 green tea bag

½ cup (125 mL) boiling water

2 cups (500 mL) frozen pineapple chunks

1 cup (250 mL) baby spinach

½ banana, thinly sliced

½ avocado, pitted and peeled

2 tsp (10 mL) honey

TO SERVE

½ banana, thinly sliced

1 cup (250 mL) raspberries

¼ cup (60 mL) unsalted dry roasted almonds, chopped

1 Place the tea bag in a large mug and pour in the boiling water. Steep the tea bag for exactly 3 minutes. Discard the tea bag.

2 Place the tea, pineapple, spinach, banana, avocado and honey in the blender and blend until thick and smooth. Divide the smoothie between two bowls.

3 To serve, top each smoothie bowl with the banana slices, raspberries and almonds. Serve immediately.

> **TOBY'S TIPS**
>
> Swap the raspberries for strawberries, blackberries or blueberries, or use a combo of berries.
>
> Use frozen pineapple chunks or cube fresh pineapple and freeze in a resealable bag.

Grape Oatmeal Cups

SERVES 6

SERVING SIZE
2 oatmeal cups

IMMUNE-
BOOSTING
FOODS: ②

Instead of a bowl of oatmeal, whip up your oats in handheld baked cups. This easy breakfast is quick to serve to kids with a glass of milk before school, and great to grab and go during a busy work week.

12-cup muffin pan lined with paper cups and coated with nonstick cooking spray

3 cups (750 mL) gluten-free large-flake (old-fashioned) rolled oats

¼ cup (60 mL) unsalted sunflower seeds

1 tsp (5 mL) baking powder

1 tsp (5 mL) ground cinnamon

½ tsp (2 mL) salt

1½ cups (375 mL) nonfat milk

2 large eggs, beaten

¼ cup (60 mL) pure maple syrup

2 tbsp (30 mL) unsalted butter, melted

1 tsp (5 mL) vanilla extract

1½ cups (375 mL) red or green seedless grapes, quartered

PREHEAT THE OVEN TO 350°F (180°C)

1 In a medium bowl, mix together the oats, sunflower seeds, baking powder, cinnamon and salt.

2 In a large bowl, whisk together the milk, eggs, maple syrup, butter and vanilla extract.

3 Mix the dry ingredients into the wet ingredients until well combined. Fold in 1 cup (250 mL) of the grapes until evenly distributed.

4 Using a ¼ cup (60 mL), scoop the batter into each of the twelve muffin cups. Tap the muffin pan a few times on the countertop to release any air bubbles. Divide the remaining ½ cup (125 mL) grapes among the twelve cups.

5 Bake until the edges of the oat cups are slightly browned and a tester inserted into the center of one or two cups comes out clean, 45 to 50 minutes.

6 Remove the muffin pan from the oven and let cool for 15 minutes before transferring the oat cups to a wire rack to cool completely. Store at room temperature for up to 5 days.

> **TOBY'S TIP** | For a creative twist, use ¾ cup (175 mL) seedless grapes, quartered, and ¾ cup (175 mL) strawberries, stems removed and thinly sliced.

Poached Pear Yogurt Bowl

SERVES 4

SERVING SIZE
1 bowl

IMMUNE-
BOOSTING
FOODS: ④

How about cooked fruit for breakfast? This warm poached pear complements the cool and creamy Greek yogurt, which is topped with nuts and seeds for some crunch.

2 pears, cored and quartered

1½ cups (375 mL) 100% pomegranate juice

1½ cups (375 mL) water

2 tbsp (30 mL) pure maple syrup

3 cinnamon sticks, halved

2 cups (500 mL) nonfat vanilla-flavored Greek yogurt

¼ cup (60 mL) unsalted sunflower seeds

¼ cup (60 mL) raw or unsalted dry roasted almonds, coarsely chopped

1 In a large saucepan, add the pears, pomegranate juice and water. If the pears are not fully covered by the liquid, add additional water. Add the maple syrup and cinnamon sticks and stir to combine. Bring to a boil over high heat, then reduce the heat to low and simmer until the pears are fork-tender, about 30 minutes. Remove the pot from the heat and let cool for 10 minutes. Remove the cinnamon sticks and discard.

2 To assemble, spoon ½ cup (125 mL) of the yogurt in each of four bowls. Place 2 pear slices with the poaching juice over the yogurt and sprinkle with 1 tbsp (15 mL) of the sunflower seeds and 1 tbsp (15 mL) of the almonds. Serve immediately.

TOBY'S TIPS

Swap the pomegranate juice for 100% cranberry juice.

The poached pears can be made in advance and stored in a covered container with the juice for up to 4 days in the refrigerator. Reheat the pears with juice in the microwave on High for about 1 minute until warmed through.

Tropical Oatmeal

Oatmeal is an easy, healthy breakfast dish that you can whip up in minutes. Even better — oats are an immune-boosting food! Pair it with antioxidant-filled fruit, like the tropical fruit in this recipe, and you've got an immune-boosting match made in oatmeal heaven.

2 cups (500 mL) gluten-free large-flake (old-fashioned) rolled oats

2 cups (500 mL) unsweetened coconut milk

2 cups (500 mL) water

1 tbsp (15 mL) honey

1 cup (250 mL) fresh or frozen and thawed mango chunks

1 cup (250 mL) fresh or frozen and thawed pineapple chunks

4 tsp (20 mL) unsweetened shredded coconut

1 In a medium saucepan, stir together the oats, coconut milk, water and honey and bring to a boil over high heat. Reduce the heat to medium-low and simmer, stirring occasionally, until the oats begin to soften and the liquid thickens, about 7 minutes. Add the mango and pineapple and stir to combine. Remove the pot from the heat.

2 Divide the oatmeal among four bowls and top each bowl with 1 tsp (5 mL) of the shredded coconut. Serve warm.

> **TOBY'S TIP** | Use unsweetened canned pineapple chunks in place of the fresh or frozen pineapple. It's a great swap and using the juice in the can in place of the honey is another way to naturally sweeten the oatmeal!

SERVES 4

SERVING SIZE
About 1¼ cups (300 mL)

IMMUNE-BOOSTING FOODS: ①

Spinach and Mushroom Egg Bake

SERVES 6

SERVING SIZE
1 slice

IMMUNE-
BOOSTING
FOODS: ③

Meal prep this dish for an easy, healthy breakfast. I like to keep individual servings ready to reheat. In the morning, my kids just heat it in the microwave and eat it before they start their first class.

8-inch (20 cm) square glass baking dish coated with nonstick cooking spray

2 tbsp (30 mL) olive oil

1 sweet onion, chopped

8 oz (250 g) mushrooms, thinly sliced

3 cloves garlic, minced

3 cups (750 mL) baby spinach, packed

¼ cup (60 mL) grated Parmesan cheese

6 large eggs

½ cup (125 mL) low-fat (1%) milk

½ tsp (2 mL) dried thyme

½ tsp (2 mL) dried rosemary

½ tsp (2 mL) salt

¼ tsp (1 mL) ground black pepper

PREHEAT THE OVEN TO 350°F (180°C)

1 In a large skillet or sauté pan, heat the olive oil over medium heat. When the oil is shimmering, add the onion, mushrooms and garlic and cook until soft and fragrant, about 5 minutes. Add the spinach and cook until wilted, about 2 minutes.

2 Spoon the cooked vegetables onto the bottom of the prepared baking dish. Sprinkle the vegetables with the Parmesan cheese.

3 In a medium bowl, whisk together the eggs, milk, thyme, rosemary, salt and pepper. Pour the egg mixture into the baking dish over the vegetables and cheese. Bake until set and the top is slightly browned, about 35 minutes.

4 Remove the dish from the oven and let cool for 10 minutes. Cut into six equal pieces and serve warm.

TOBY'S TIP | To freeze individual servings, cool completely. Transfer to individual freezer-safe resealable containers and freeze for up to 2 months. To reheat, thaw in the refrigerator overnight then transfer to a microwave-safe dish. Heat in the microwave on High for 45 seconds.

Breakfast Quesadilla WITH
EGG, SPINACH, RED PEPPER AND BACON

SERVES 4

SERVING SIZE
1 quesadilla

IMMUNE-
BOOSTING
FOODS: ③

Although this is a breakfast menu item, sometimes I enjoy serving it as breakfast for dinner. It's a wholesome savory meal that always hits the spot, whether it's morning or night.

Medium skillet coated with nonstick cooking spray

3 slices nitrite-free bacon

4 large eggs

1/8 tsp (0.5 mL) salt

1/8 tsp (0.5 mL) ground black pepper

1 tbsp (15 mL) olive oil or canola oil

1 clove garlic, minced

1 red bell pepper, seeded and chopped

2 cups (500 mL) baby spinach

Four 8-inch (20 cm) whole wheat tortillas

1 cup (250 mL) part-skim shredded mozzarella cheese

1 cup (250 mL) salsa

1 Heat the prepared skillet over medium heat. When the oil is shimmering, add the bacon and cook until crispy, about 6 minutes, turning occasionally. Transfer the bacon to a paper towel to drain. Use a paper towel to wipe the skillet clean. Let the bacon cool slightly, then chop into 1/2-inch (1 cm) pieces and set aside.

2 In a medium bowl, whisk together the eggs, salt and black pepper.

3 Coat the same skillet with nonstick cooking spray and place over medium heat. When the oil is shimmering, pour the egg mixture into the center of the skillet. Cook the eggs, using a rubber spatula to push them gently from the edges into the center of the skillet until they are set, 4 to 5 minutes. Spoon the scrambled eggs onto a clean plate, cover with a paper towel to keep warm and set aside. Use a paper towel to wipe the skillet clean.

4 Heat the oil in the same skillet over medium heat. When the oil is shimmering, add the garlic and cook until fragrant, 30 seconds. Add the red pepper and cook until slightly softened, 3 to 4 minutes. Add the spinach and allow to wilt, about 2 minutes more. Spoon the vegetable mixture onto a clean plate. Use a paper towel to wipe the skillet clean.

5 Coat the skillet with nonstick cooking spray and place over medium heat. When the oil is shimmering, add 1 tortilla. Onto one half of the tortilla, sprinkle 2 tbsp (30 mL) of the cheese and layer one-quarter of the egg mixture, one-quarter of the vegetable mixture and one-quarter of the bacon pieces over the cheese. Top with another 2 tbsp (30 mL) of the cheese. Fold the empty half of the tortilla over the filling.

Continue cooking for about 3 minutes and
then, using a spatula, carefully flip the quesadilla
and cook until the tortilla is slightly toasted and
browned, 3 minutes more. Place the quesadilla on a
clean plate and repeat for the remaining 3 tortillas.

6 Using a pizza cutter or sharp knife, slice the
quesadilla into thirds. Serve immediately with
$1/4$ cup (60 mL) salsa on the side.

TOBY'S TIP For a lower-fat version, swap the bacon
for turkey bacon or leave the bacon out
completely if you wish.

Almond Butter and Pear Toast

SERVING SIZE
1 toast

This speedy breakfast can be ready in about 10 minutes. Even better, you're getting a well-balanced breakfast with three food groups — grains, protein and fruit — plus boosting your immune system at the same time.

IMMUNE-BOOSTING FOODS: ②

¼ cup (60 mL) almond butter

2 tbsp (30 mL) water

1 tsp (5 mL) pure maple syrup

¼ tsp (1 mL) ground cinnamon

2 slices 100% whole wheat bread, toasted

½ pear, cored and thinly sliced

2 tsp (10 mL) unsalted roasted almonds, chopped

1 In a small saucepan, add the almond butter, water, maple syrup and cinnamon and place over high heat. Bring the mixture to a boil while whisking constantly. Reduce the heat to low and continue whisking until the almond butter mixture softens, about 1 minute. Remove the saucepan from the heat and let cool for 5 minutes.

2 On each of two slices of bread, spread about 2 tbsp (30 mL) of the almond butter mixture and top with half of the pear slices. Sprinkle each slice with 1 tsp (5 mL) of the chopped almonds. Serve immediately.

> **TOBY'S TIP**
> To find out if a pear is ready to eat, "check the neck." Use your thumb and forefinger to gently press on the neck of the pear. If it gives slightly, it's ripe!

Chocolate Chip Walnut Muffins

These better-for-you muffins use ingredients that are easy to find, like whole wheat flour, low-fat milk and Greek yogurt. Plus they provide immune-boosting walnuts.

SERVES 12

SERVING SIZE
1 muffin

IMMUNE-BOOSTING FOODS: ①

12-cup muffin pan coated with nonstick cooking spray

1½ cups (375 mL) unbleached all-purpose flour

1 cup (250 mL) 100% whole wheat flour

2 tsp (10 mL) baking powder

½ tsp (2 mL) baking soda

½ tsp (2 mL) salt

1 cup (250 mL) low-fat (1%) milk

½ cup (125 mL) nonfat plain Greek yogurt

½ cup (125 mL) light brown sugar

¼ cup (60 mL) canola oil

¼ cup (60 mL) unsalted butter, melted

1 large egg, beaten

1 tsp (5 mL) vanilla extract

¾ cup (175 mL) raw or unsalted dry roasted walnuts, coarsely chopped

¾ cup (175 mL) semi-sweet or dark chocolate chips

PREHEAT OVEN TO 350°F (180°C)

1 In a medium bowl, sift together the all-purpose flour, whole wheat flour, baking powder, baking soda and salt. In a separate medium bowl, whisk together the milk, yogurt, brown sugar, oil, butter, egg and vanilla.

2 Gently fold the dry mixture into the wet mixture with as few strokes as possible until moistened. Do not overmix. Add the walnuts and chocolate chips and fold until just combined.

3 Divide the batter evenly between the twelve muffin cups. Tap the muffin pan several times on the counter to get rid of any air bubbles.

4 Bake in the center of the oven until a tester inserted into two muffins comes out clean, 18 to 20 minutes. Remove from the oven and let cool for 2 to 3 minutes in the pan. Remove the muffins from pan and finish cooling on a wire rack for 10 minutes.

5 Serve immediately or store at room temperature in a sealable container for up to 5 days.

> **TOBY'S TIP** | For a well-balanced diet, pair these muffins with immune-boosting strawberries or an orange and a glass or milk.

TOBY'S
TIP

Swap the raisins for dried tart cherries or dried cranberries.

Nut and Seed Breakfast Cookies

These breakfast cookies are brimming with immune-boosting ingredients: almonds, walnuts and sunflower seeds. Meal prep these cookies on Sunday and enjoy them throughout your busy work week. Pair with a glass of milk, yogurt or fresh fruit.

IMMUNE-BOOSTING FOODS: ③

2 baking sheets lined with parchment paper

1½ cups (375 mL) unbleached all-purpose flour

1 cup (250 mL) large flake (old-fashioned) rolled oats

1 tsp (5 mL) ground cinnamon

1 tsp (5 mL) baking soda

½ tsp (2 mL) salt

1 cup (250 mL) almond butter

½ cup (125 mL) unsweetened applesauce

6 tbsp (90 mL) pure maple syrup

2 eggs, beaten

1 tsp (5 mL) vanilla extract

¼ cup (60 mL) raw walnuts, coarsely chopped

¼ cup (60 mL) raw almonds, coarsely chopped

¼ cup (60 mL) unsalted sunflower seeds

½ cup (125 mL) raisins

PREHEAT THE OVEN TO 350°F (180°C)

1 In a medium bowl, using a wooden spoon, mix together the all-purpose flour, oats, cinnamon, baking soda and salt.

2 In a large bowl, whisk together the almond butter, applesauce and maple syrup until well combined. Add the eggs and vanilla extract and whisk until smooth.

3 Gently fold the dry ingredients into the wet ingredients and stir until just combined. Fold in the walnuts, almonds, sunflower seeds and raisins, evenly distributing throughout the dough.

4 Scoop out ¼ cup (60 mL) of the dough and, using clean hands, roll into a ball. Place onto a prepared baking sheet and gently press down on the top to flatten slightly. Repeat with the rest of the batter, leaving about 1 inch (2.5 cm) between the cookies.

5 Bake for 18 minutes, until the cookies are golden brown but soft and a tester inserted into the center of two cookies comes out clean. Transfer the cookies to a wire rack and let cool for about 10 minutes.

6 Serve warm or, once the cookies have completely cooled, store, covered, at room temperature for up to 5 days. Cookies can also be placed in a sealable bag and stored in the freezer for up to 2 months.

Orange Greek Yogurt Pancakes WITH STRAWBERRY SAUCE

SERVES 6

SERVING SIZE
2 pancakes plus
$^{1}/_{4}$ cup (60 mL)
sauce

IMMUNE-
BOOSTING
FOODS: ②

Although this recipe uses strawberries, other berries like blueberries, raspberries and blackberries also have immune-boosting benefits and can always be used instead of or together with the strawberries.

Griddle or large skillet coated with nonstick cooking spray

STRAWBERRY SAUCE

4 cups (1 L) fresh or frozen and thawed strawberries, thinly sliced

2 tbsp (30 mL) pure maple syrup

Juice of $^{1}/_{2}$ lemon

PANCAKES

1 cup (250 mL) unbleached all-purpose flour

1 cup (250 mL) whole wheat flour or white whole wheat flour

$1^{1}/_{2}$ tsp (7 mL) baking powder

$^{1}/_{2}$ tsp (2 mL) baking soda

$^{1}/_{2}$ tsp (2 mL) salt

1 cup (250 mL) nonfat milk

$^{1}/_{2}$ cup (125 mL) nonfat plain Greek yogurt

Zest and juice of 1 orange

2 tbsp (30 mL) canola oil

2 tbsp (30 mL) light brown sugar

2 large eggs, beaten

1 TO MAKE THE STRAWBERRY SAUCE: In a medium saucepan, heat the strawberries, maple syrup and lemon juice over high heat and bring the mixture to a boil. Lower the heat to low and simmer, stirring occasionally, until the strawberries have softened, 20 to 25 minutes. Remove the saucepan from the heat and let the sauce cool for at least 10 minutes in order to slightly thicken.

2 TO MAKE THE PANCAKES: In a medium bowl, sift the all-purpose flour, whole wheat flour, baking powder, baking soda and salt.

3 In a separate medium bowl, whisk together the milk, yogurt, orange juice and zest, canola oil and brown sugar until well combined. Add the eggs and whisk until incorporated.

4 Pour the flour mixture into the wet mixture and gently stir them together, mixing until just combined. Do not overmix.

5 Heat the prepared griddle or large skillet over medium heat. Scoop a heaping $^{1}/_{4}$ cup (60 mL) of batter onto the griddle or skillet, leaving room between cakes. Cook until the top is bubbly and the edges are set, 3 to 4 minutes, then flip over and cook for another 2 to 3 minutes until golden brown. Remove and place on a clean plate. Repeat with remaining batter to make a total of twelve pancakes.

6 TO ASSEMBLE: Stack two pancakes on a plate and top with ¹/₄ cup (60 mL) of the strawberry sauce. Repeat with the remaining pancakes and sauce. Serve warm.

TOBY'S
TIP | Eggs come in various sizes such as medium, large, extra-large and jumbo. For cooking and baking, use large eggs unless otherwise specified.

TOBY'S TIPS

Swap the whole wheat bread for challah for a fun spin on this dish.

Meal prep by cooking the berry mixture up to 3 days in advance. Store in a sealed container in the refrigerator and rewarm before serving.

Berry-Stuffed French Toast

This berry-filled breakfast is brimming with anthocyanins, which are natural plant chemicals that help fight inflammation and act as an antioxidant. All berries provide anthocyanins and can help boost your immune response. So enjoy berries at any meal or snack!

SERVING SIZE
1 stuffed
French toast

IMMUNE-
BOOSTING
FOODS: ③

Large skillet coated with nonstick cooking spray

FILLING

1 cup (250 mL) fresh or frozen and thawed strawberries, diced

1/2 cup (125 mL) fresh or frozen and thawed blueberries

1/2 cup (125 mL) fresh or frozen and thawed raspberries

1/4 cup (60 mL) water

2 tbsp (30 mL) 100% maple syrup

1 tbsp (15 mL) lemon juice

1/4 tsp (1 mL) ground cinnamon

FRENCH TOAST

1 1/2 cups (375 mL) nonfat milk

4 large eggs

1 tbsp (15 mL) vanilla extract

1/2 tsp (2 mL) ground cinnamon

Nonstick cooking spray

8 slices 100% whole wheat bread

TO ASSEMBLE

1 cup (250 mL) nonfat vanilla-flavored Greek yogurt

1 tbsp (15 mL) confectioners' sugar

1 TO MAKE THE FILLING: In a small saucepan, add the strawberries, blueberries, raspberries, water, maple syrup, lemon juice and cinnamon and bring to a boil over high heat. Once boiling, reduce the heat to medium-low and simmer, stirring occasionally, until the berries have broken down and the mixture has thickened, about 20 minutes. Remove the saucepan from the heat and let cool for 10 minutes.

2 TO MAKE THE FRENCH TOAST: In a medium bowl, whisk together the milk, eggs, vanilla and cinnamon. Heat the prepared skillet over medium-low heat.

3 Soak 3 or 4 slices of the bread in the mixture, turning to moisten both sides. Place the slices of the soaked bread in the heated skillet. Cook until the bottom of the French toast is golden brown, 3 to 4 minutes. Flip and cook until the second side is golden brown, 3 to 4 minutes. Remove the French toast to a clean plate and cover with aluminum foil to keep warm. Repeat with the remaining slices of bread.

4 TO ASSEMBLE: Place 1 slice of French toast on a plate. Spoon 1/4 cup (60 mL) of the yogurt in the center of the French toast and top with 3 tbsp (45 mL) of the berry mixture. Place another slice of French toast over the top. Repeat to create the remaining 3 stuffed French toasts. Sprinkle confectioners' sugar evenly over the top and serve warm.

Whole Wheat Cranberry-Orange Loaf

Enjoy a delicious slice of this fruit-filled loaf. Cranberries are an excellent source of the antioxidants vitamins C and E and can be a delicious part of your immune-boosting diet.

9- by 5-inch (23 by 12.5 cm) loaf pan coated with nonstick cooking spray

Juice of 1 navel orange and five 1-inch (2.5 cm) slices of orange peel

1½ cups (375 mL) dried cranberries

1 cup (250 mL) boiling water

1 cup (250 mL) unbleached all-purpose flour

1 cup (250 mL) 100% whole wheat flour

1½ tsp (7 mL) baking powder

½ tsp (2 mL) baking soda

½ tsp (2 mL) salt

½ cup (125 mL) canola oil

½ cup (125 mL) low-fat (1%) milk

⅓ cup (75 mL) pure maple syrup

¼ cup (60 mL) light brown sugar

2 large eggs, beaten

1 tsp (5 mL) vanilla extract

1 Add the orange peel and cranberries to a medium bowl and cover with the boiling water. Set aside and let soak for 1 hour.

2 Preheat the oven to 350°F (180°C).

3 In a medium bowl, sift together the all-purpose flour, whole wheat flour, baking powder, baking soda and salt.

4 In a separate medium bowl, whisk together the canola oil, milk, maple syrup and brown sugar. Whisk in the orange juice, eggs and vanilla.

5 Drain the cranberries and discard the orange peel.

6 Add the dry mixture to the wet mixture and stir until just combined. Gently fold in the cranberries until evenly distributed in the batter.

7 Pour the batter into the prepared loaf pan and use a spatula to even out the top. Bake until a tester inserted into the loaf comes out clean, 50 to 55 minutes. Remove from the oven and let cool for 10 minutes. Turn out onto a wire rack to cool completely.

8 Cut the loaf into eight equal slices. Serve immediately or store, covered, for up to 5 days. The loaf can also be stored in the freezer for up to 2 months.

TOBY'S TIP | You can also make this with 1 cup (250 mL) of fresh cranberries instead of dried and orange zest instead of orange peel. No need to soak the cranberries before using.

CHAPTER 4

SMOOTHIES AND BEVERAGES

Immune-Boosting Green Tea Smoothie

SERVING SIZE
1 cup (250 mL)

IMMUNE-
BOOSTING
FOODS: ③

Smoothies aren't just for fruits. This smoothie provides fruits, vegetables and immune-boosting green tea. The fruits and vegetables also deliver a variety of antioxidants and phytonutrients, which can help boost your body's defenses.

Blender

1 green teabag

1 cup (250 mL) boiling water

1 cup (250 mL) frozen pineapple chunks

1 frozen banana

½ cup (125 mL) packed baby spinach

½ cup (125 mL) frozen cauliflower florets

2 tsp (10 mL) fresh lemon juice

1 Add the teabag to a mug and pour in the boiling water. Let the tea steep for exactly 3 minutes. Remove the teabag and discard, and let the tea cool for 10 minutes.

2 Blend the green tea, pineapple, banana, spinach, cauliflower and lemon juice in the blender on High until smooth, 30 to 45 seconds.

3 Pour into two glasses and serve immediately.

> **TOBY'S TIP** | When steeping green tea set a timer. Steep for exactly 3 minutes to get the most flavor without it getting bitter.

Pineapple-Turmeric Smoothie

SERVES 2

SERVING SIZE
About 1 cup
(250 mL)

IMMUNE-
BOOSTING
FOODS: ②

Turmeric is a wonderful immune-boosting ingredient, but it has a strong flavor. In this smoothie, the orange juice, pineapple and mango complement and mellow the flavor for a refreshing morning bevie.

Blender

1 cup (250 mL) orange juice

½ cup (125 mL) coconut milk

½ tsp (2 mL) ground turmeric

1 cup (250 mL) frozen pineapple chunks

1 cup (250 mL) frozen mango chunks

1 pitted date

1 Blend the orange juice, coconut milk and turmeric in a blender on High until well incorporated, about 20 seconds.

2 Add the pineapple, mango and date into the blender and blend on High until smooth, 30 to 45 seconds.

3 Pour into two glasses and serve immediately.

> **TOBY'S TIP** | Swap the coconut milk for unsweetened almond or soy milk.

Pear Ginger Smoothie

One of my favorite things about smoothies is that you can blend and take it to go. I keep a few insulated to-go cups in my kitchen so I always have a clean one ready.

SERVING SIZE
1 cup (250 mL)

IMMUNE-
BOOSTING
FOODS: ③

Blender

1 pear, cored and cut into large chunks

1 frozen banana

½ cup (125 mL) almond milk or nonfat milk

¼ cup (60 mL) reduced-fat (2%) plain Greek yogurt

2 tbsp (30 mL) almond butter

¾ tsp (3 mL) ground ginger

½ tsp (2 mL) vanilla extract

¼ tsp (1 mL) ground cinnamon

1 Add the pear, banana, milk, yogurt, almond butter, ginger, vanilla extract and cinnamon to the blender and blend on High until smooth, 30 to 45 seconds.

2 Pour into two glasses and serve immediately.

> **TOBY'S TIP** | If you like your smoothie very gingery, increase the ground ginger to 1 tsp (5 mL).

Grape Slushie

There's no need to buy a slushie with tons of added sugar when you can easily make your own. This slushie uses only the natural sweetness of the grapes mixed with a touch of tart flavor from the lime.

Blender

2 cups (500 mL) frozen seedless red grapes

½ cup (125 mL) water

Juice of ½ lime

SERVING SIZE
¾ cup (175 mL)

IMMUNE-BOOSTING FOODS: ①

1 Add the grapes, water and lime juice to the blender and blend on High until smooth, about 1 minute. Using a spatula, scrape down the sides of the blender and blend for about 30 seconds more.

2 Spoon the slushie into two glasses and serve immediately with a straw.

TOBY'S TIP | To freeze the grapes, place them in a single layer on a rimmed baking sheet and put the pan in the freezer for at least 6 hours until frozen. Transfer the frozen grapes to sealable plastic bags and label them with the "use by" date of up to 2 months.

Strawberry-Oat Smoothie

SERVES 2

SERVING SIZE
About 1 cup
(250 mL)

IMMUNE-
BOOSTING
FOODS: ③

My kids love when I deliver morning smoothies to them when they're in their online classes. This smoothie has become a favorite in my household, and as a mom, I'm happy they're getting not only a nutritious meal but also three immune-boosting foods.

Blender

1 cup (250 mL) nonfat milk

¼ cup (60 mL) quick-cooking rolled oats

1 cup (250 mL) frozen strawberries

1 frozen banana

¼ cup (60 mL) reduced-fat (2%) plain Greek yogurt

2 tsp (10 mL) honey

½ tsp (3 mL) vanilla extract

1 Add the milk and oats to the blender and let sit for 15 minutes.

2 Add the strawberries, banana, yogurt, honey and vanilla to the blender with the oats and blend on High until smooth, 30 to 45 seconds.

3 Pour into two glasses and serve immediately.

> **TOBY'S TIP** | Make sure to wait at least 15 minutes before adding the other ingredients to the blender. This allows enough time for the oats to soak up the milk and blend beautifully into your smoothie.

Golden Milk

Turmeric blended with milk has been part of Indian culture for many centuries. It's called *haldi doodh* in Hindi and is very popular to this day. You may also see it listed on café menus as "turmeric latte." Luckily, you can make your own warming cup of Golden Milk in just a few minutes and enjoy it in your own kitchen.

SERVING SIZE
1 cup (250 mL)

IMMUNE-
BOOSTING
FOODS: ③

1 tbsp (15 mL) almond butter

2 tsp (10 mL) honey

½ tsp (2 mL) ground ginger

¼ tsp (1 mL) vanilla extract

¼ tsp (1 mL) ground cinnamon

¼ tsp (1 mL) ground turmeric

Small pinch of ground black pepper

1 cup (250 mL) unsweetened coconut milk

1 cup (250 mL) unsweetened almond milk

1 In a small saucepan over low heat, whisk the almond butter, honey, ginger, vanilla, cinnamon, turmeric and black pepper until combined, about 30 seconds. Add ¼ cup (60 mL) of coconut milk and whisk vigorously to incorporate the spice mixture into the liquid, about 15 seconds. Increase the heat to medium and slowly whisk in the remaining ¾ cup (175 mL) coconut milk and the almond milk.

2 Pour into two mugs and serve immediately.

> **TOBY'S TIP** Don't leave out the black pepper! Adding black pepper to this beverage helps increase the body's absorption of curcumin — the potent anti-inflammatory found in turmeric.

Citrus Spritzer

SERVES 4

SERVING SIZE
1 cup (250 mL)

IMMUNE-
BOOSTING
FOODS: ①

Whip up your own festive "soda" for an anytime treat. That way you have full control over the ingredients, including the added sugar. This fun fizzy drink combines three citrus fruits, which provides a boatload of vitamin C — perfect to help boost your immune system.

Six 1-inch (2.5 cm) slices of peel and juice of 2 navel oranges

Four 1-inch (2.5 cm) slices of peel and juice of 1/2 grapefruit

Four 1-inch (2.5 cm) slices of peel and juice of 1 lemon

1 tbsp (15 mL) honey

2 cups (500 mL) ice

2 cups (500 mL) seltzer

1 Blend the orange juice, grapefruit juice, lemon juice and honey in a blender on High until incorporated, about 20 seconds.

2 Fill a pitcher with the ice and then the sparkling water. Add the blender mixture and the orange, grapefruit, and lemon peels and stir with a wooden spoon to combine.

3 Place the pitcher in the refrigerator to allow the flavors to blend, about 15 minutes.

4 Pour into four glasses and serve immediately.

TOBY'S TIPS

You may find different varieties of oranges and grapefruits at the store, like Cara Cara or blood oranges or pink or red grapefruit. Give them a try for a twist on the citrus flavor.

Add fresh mint to the pitcher for more flavor.

Strawberry Limeade

Make your own fruit-flavored sparkling "soda" using fresh fruit and herbs. It's a flavorful way to add fluids to your day and help boost your immune system.

2 cups (500 mL) fresh or frozen and thawed strawberries, quartered

½ cup (125 mL) fresh lime juice (about 4 limes)

¼ cup (60 mL) honey

2 cups (500 mL) ice

4 cups (1 L) sparkling water

¼ cup (60 mL) packed mint leaves

SERVING SIZE
1½ cups
(375 mL)

IMMUNE-
BOOSTING
FOODS: ①

1 Place the strawberries, lime juice and honey in a blender and blend for 30 to 45 seconds on High until smooth.

2 Fill a medium pitcher with ice and the strawberry mixture and then add the sparkling water. Stir gently with a wooden spoon. Add the mint leaves and stir to combine. Transfer the pitcher to the refrigerator and chill for at least 20 minutes to allow the flavors to blend.

3 Divide the chilled drink among four tall glasses and serve.

> **TOBY'S TIPS**
>
> Instead of mint, use basil.
>
> To get the most juice out of your limes, using clean hands roll the limes several times while pressing down on them on a flat surface before cutting them.

CHAPTER 5

SNACKS AND MINI MEALS

Garlic Dip

What's the best way to use lots of garlic? This immune-boosting dip! You'll certainly get a garlicky kick at the end, but the cooling Greek yogurt and tart lemons balance the flavor beautifully.

Blender or food processor

12 garlic cloves, minced

½ tsp (2 mL) kosher salt

½ cup (125 mL) olive oil

1 cup (250 mL) nonfat plain Greek yogurt

Juice of 2 lemons

1 Place the garlic cloves and kosher salt in a blender or food processor and blend until smooth. With the blender or food processor running, slowly drizzle in the olive oil until combined. Add the yogurt and lemon juice and blend on High until well combined, about 30 seconds.

2 Serve immediately or cover and store in the refrigerator for up to 4 days.

> **TOBY'S TIP** | Serve the dip with cut vegetables, like celery, carrots and cucumbers, or with whole grain pretzels.

Yogurt "Caramel" Dip
WITH PEARS

Many of the recipes in this book call for cinnamon, which I like to use not only for its warming flavor but also because it has been shown to have antioxidant, antibiotic and anti-inflammatory properties. More research is still needed to better understand the role of cinnamon in our diets, but in the meantime it's easy to enjoy this delicious spice.

$1/2$ cup (125 mL) almond butter

$1/2$ cup (125 mL) nonfat plain Greek yogurt

2 tbsp (30 mL) pure maple syrup

$1/2$ tsp (2 mL) ground cinnamon

4 medium pears, cored and sliced

1 In a small microwave-safe bowl, add the almond butter and microwave on High for 30 seconds or until softened. Set aside and let cool for 5 minutes.

2 In a medium bowl, mix together the almond butter, Greek yogurt, maple syrup and cinnamon until well combined.

3 Scoop $1/4$ cup (60 mL) of the dip into four small bowls and serve each alongside the slices of 1 pear.

TOBY'S TIPS | Use a combination of apples and pears for dipping or replace the pears with sliced apples or bananas.

There are numerous varieties of pears you will find at the store. My favorite is the Red Anjou, but you can give each a try and see which you like best.

Strawberry Kiwi Almond Yogurt Bark

SERVING SIZE
4 pieces

IMMUNE-
BOOSTING
FOODS: ④

If you're looking to satisfy your sweet tooth, this yogurt bark is your answer. All of the ingredients in this recipe help boost your immune system. Kiwi is a colorful fruit brimming with the antioxidants C and E, both of which play a role in a healthy immune system.

Rimmed baking sheet lined with parchment paper

2 cups (500 g) nonfat vanilla-flavored Greek yogurt

Zest of 1 orange

8 strawberries, stems removed and diced

2 kiwifruit, peeled and diced

1/2 cup (125 g) unsalted dry roasted almonds, coarsely chopped

1 In a medium bowl, add the yogurt and stir in half of the zest. Spoon the yogurt mixture onto the prepared baking sheet and use a spatula to spread it evenly to the edges. It should be about 1/2 inch (1 cm) thick.

2 Evenly sprinkle the yogurt with the strawberries, kiwis and almonds, and then dust the remaining zest over the yogurt.

3 Place the baking sheet in the freezer for at least 4 hours or until the yogurt sets. Gently break the yogurt bark into twenty-four pieces. Store in a sealable container in the freezer for up to 2 weeks.

> **TOBY'S TIP** | Swap the almonds for pistachios, peanuts, cashews or even sunflower seeds.

Nut and Seed Clusters

Toss fiber-filled nuts and seeds in maple syrup and bake in the oven for a healthy, crunchy snack just waiting to be devoured. Pure maple syrup binds the clusters together and provides small amounts of vitamins and minerals, too.

Baking sheet lined with parchment paper or silicone mat

⅓ cup (75 mL) pure maple syrup

Zest of 1 orange

1 tsp (5 mL) vanilla extract

⅛ tsp (0.5 mL) kosher salt

½ cup (125 mL) raw sunflower seeds

½ cup (125 mL) raw almonds, coarsely chopped

½ cup (125 mL) raw walnuts, coarsely chopped

2 tbsp (30 mL) poppy seeds

SERVES 6

SERVING SIZE
2 pieces

IMMUNE-BOOSTING FOODS: ④

PREHEAT THE OVEN TO 350°F (180°C)

1 In a small bowl, whisk together the maple syrup, orange zest, vanilla and salt.

2 In a medium bowl, combine the sunflower seeds, almonds, walnuts and poppy seeds. Pour the syrup mixture over the nuts and seeds and toss to coat.

3 Place about 2 tbsp (30 mL) of the mixture onto the prepared baking sheet, leaving about 1 inch (2.5 cm) between each cluster for a total of twelve clusters. Bake until the clusters are slightly browned, about 15 minutes. Remove the baking sheet from the oven and let cool for 10 to 15 minutes.

4 Remove the clusters to a plate and serve. Clusters can also be stored in a sealable container for up to 5 days at room temperature.

TOBY'S TIPS

Enjoy these clusters as a snack or crumble them over yogurt or oatmeal for a granola-like topping.

Raw nuts and seeds always come without salt. If you cannot find the nuts or seeds raw for this dish, then look for an unsalted dry roasted variety.

Swap any of the nuts in the recipe for pistachios or cashews — or just use 1½ cups (375 mL) of whatever nut and seed combination you wish.

Roasted Spiced Chickpeas

These spiced chickpeas are made with a combination of immune-boosting turmeric and ginger. Not only do you get fantastic flavors in this delicious snack, but you are also helping to keep your immune system in tip-top shape.

SERVING SIZE
¼ cup (60 mL)

IMMUNE-BOOSTING FOODS: ③

Rimmed baking sheet with coated with nonstick cooking spray

1 can (14 to 19 oz/398 to 540 mL) low-sodium chickpeas, drained and rinsed

1 tbsp (15 mL) olive oil

¼ tsp (1 mL) salt

⅛ tsp (0.5 mL) ground black pepper

½ tsp (2 mL) ground turmeric

½ tsp (2 mL) ground cumin

½ tsp (2 mL) ground ginger

PREHEAT THE OVEN TO 375°F (190°C)

1 Place the rinsed chickpeas on a clean towel and gently fold the towel over to dry.

2 In a medium bowl, add the chickpeas, oil, salt and pepper. Toss to combine.

3 Place in a single layer on the prepared baking sheet and bake until crispy, 30 to 40 minutes, checking to make sure the chickpeas do not burn. Remove from the oven and let cool on the baking sheet for about 10 minutes.

4 In a small bowl, combine the turmeric, cumin and ground ginger. Sprinkle over cooled chickpeas.

5 Serve immediately or store in a sealable container for up to 4 days.

> **TOBY'S TIP**
> For crispier chickpeas, dry them thoroughly after rinsing and remove the thin skin of the chickpeas.

Walnut Date Energy Bites

Bites are so easy to put together: just blend, roll, refrigerate. Once they firm up, you can pack them into single servings for quick and satisfying snacks on the go. They also make snack time easy with younger kids.

Food processor or blender

Rimmed baking sheet lined with parchment paper

1 cup (250 mL) raw or unsalted dry roasted walnuts

5 pitted dates

2 tbsp (30 mL) pure maple syrup

2 tbsp (30 mL) smooth almond butter

¼ tsp (1 mL) vanilla extract

¼ tsp (1 mL) ground cinnamon

⅛ tsp (0.5 mL) salt

½ cup (125 mL) unsweetened shredded coconut

1 In the bowl of a food processor or blender, add the walnuts, dates, maple syrup, almond butter, vanilla, cinnamon and salt. Pulse until the mixture reaches a crumbly consistency, about 1 minute. Transfer to a medium bowl.

2 On a large flat plate, add the coconut. Using clean hands, roll 1 tbsp (15 mL) of the walnut-date mixture into a 2-inch (5 cm) ball and roll it in the shredded coconut. Place the ball on the prepared baking sheet. Repeat with the remaining ingredients, making a total of twelve balls.

3 Refrigerate to allow the balls to set, at least 15 minutes before eating. Bites can be stored in a sealable container in the refrigerator for up to 5 days.

SERVING SIZE
2 bites

IMMUNE-
BOOSTING
FOODS: ②

TOBY'S TIPS | This is a great recipe to get the kids involved in the kitchen! Ask them to mold the sticky mixture into the balls.

When shopping for almond butter, make sure to read the ingredients. Look for jars made only from almonds.

Carrot Sunflower Mini Muffins

SERVES 12

SERVING SIZE
3 mini muffins

IMMUNE-BOOSTING FOODS: ②

Good things come in small packages — especially these mini muffins! The carrots add beta-carotene, which is an immune-boosting antioxidant. Pair these muffins with even more antioxidants from fresh fruit like strawberries, grapes or pineapple for a powerhouse snack.

Three 12-cup mini muffin pans coated with nonstick cooking spray

1¼ cups (300 mL) unbleached all-purpose flour

1 cup (250 mL) whole wheat flour

2 tsp (10 mL) baking powder

1 tsp (5 mL) baking soda

1 tsp (5 mL) ground cinnamon

½ tsp (2 mL) salt

⅛ tsp (0.5 mL) ground nutmeg

½ cup (125 mL) canola oil

½ cup (125 mL) 100% orange juice

¼ cup (60 mL) pure maple syrup

2 large eggs, beaten

1 tsp (5 mL) vanilla extract

2 medium carrots, peeled and grated

½ cup (125 mL) unsalted sunflower seeds

PREHEAT THE OVEN TO 375°F (190°C)

1 In a medium bowl, sift together the all-purpose flour, whole wheat flour, baking powder, baking soda, cinnamon, salt and nutmeg.

2 In a large bowl, whisk together the oil, orange juice, maple syrup, eggs and vanilla.

3 Gently fold the dry ingredients into the wet ingredients, being careful not to overmix the batter. Gently fold in the carrots and sunflower seeds to evenly distribute them throughout the batter.

4 Using a tablespoon, scoop the batter into each of the prepared thirty-six mini muffin cups. Tap the muffin pan onto the counter a few times to get rid of any bubbles.

5 Bake until the muffins are golden brown on top and a toothpick inserted in the center comes out clean, 15 to 18 minutes. Remove the pan from the oven and let cool for 10 minutes before transferring the muffins to a wire rack to finish cooling for another 10 minutes.

TOBY'S TIP Add ¼ cup (60 mL) golden raisins to the batter with the sunflower seeds for extra sweetness.

106 SNACKS AND MINI MEALS

Egg-Stuffed Bell Peppers
WITH TOMATO AND MOZZARELLA

SERVES 6

SERVING SIZE
1 pepper half

IMMUNE-
BOOSTING
FOODS: ②

Get creative in the kitchen by whipping up these egg-stuffed peppers. They're a delicious way to add immune-boosting peppers into your day. And although tomatoes aren't on my top 25 list, they provide a hefty amount of the antioxidant vitamin C, which certainly can help support your immune system.

13- by 9-inch (33 by 23 cm) glass baking dish coated with nonstick cooking spray

3 red bell peppers, cored, halved lengthwise and seeds removed

3 oz (90 g) fresh mozzarella cheese, diced into ½-inch (1 cm) cubes

2 plum (Roma) tomatoes, diced

1 tbsp (15 mL) olive oil

1 tsp (5 mL) dried parsley flakes

½ tsp (2 mL) ground oregano

¼ tsp (1 mL) salt

⅛ tsp (0.5 mL) ground black pepper

6 large eggs

2 tbsp (30 mL) shredded Parmesan cheese

PREHEAT THE OVEN TO 375°F (190°C)

1 Place the peppers cut-side up on a large microwave-safe plate. Microwave on High until tender, about 3 minutes.

2 In a medium bowl, add the mozzarella cheese and tomatoes and toss to combine. Add the oil, parsley, oregano, salt and black pepper and toss to evenly coat the cheese and tomatoes.

3 Place about 2 tbsp (30 mL) of the tomato mixture into each of the 6 red pepper halves. Carefully crack an egg into a small glass bowl and gently pour over the tomato mixture. Then place the red pepper on the prepared baking sheet cut-side up. Repeat for the remaining 5 red bell peppers. Sprinkle 1 tsp (5 mL) of the Parmesan cheese over the top of each egg. Bake until the eggs have set, about 30 minutes.

4 Remove the baking sheet from the oven and let rest for 10 minutes before serving warm.

TOBY'S TIP | Keep an eye on your eggs while they're baking. If you prefer runnier eggs, then bake for about 25 minutes. For firmer yolks, you can keep them in the oven for about 35 minutes.

Spiced Cauliflower "Popcorn"

SERVING SIZE
1 cup (250 mL)

IMMUNE-
BOOSTING
FOODS: ②

Looking for your new favorite snack food? In this dish, bite-size cauliflower florets are roasted until they're crispy, then they're mixed with savory spices. It feels like you're eating popcorn! The turmeric and cauliflower are your two immune-boosting foods in this recipe, and the turmeric provides a gorgeous yellow hue to the cauliflower.

Baking sheet coated with cooking spray

¼ cup (60 mL) olive oil

2 tbsp (30 mL) grated Parmesan cheese

2 tsp (10 mL) turmeric

2 tsp (10 mL) garlic powder

¼ tsp (1 mL) salt

2 heads cauliflower, cut into bite-size florets with the stems trimmed

PREHEAT THE OVEN TO 425°F (220°C)

1 In a small bowl, whisk together the olive oil, Parmesan cheese, turmeric, garlic powder, and salt.

2 In a large bowl, add the cauliflower and drizzle the oil mixture over the cauliflower. Toss to evenly coat.

3 Spoon the cauliflower onto the prepared baking sheet and spread in a single layer. Bake until the cauliflower is crispy, about 25 minutes, flipping halfway through. Remove the baking sheet from the oven and let cool for 10 minutes. Serve immediately.

> **TOBY'S TIP** | Purchase garlic powder verses garlic salt. Garlic powder has minimal sodium, and by having to add salt separately, you have more control over how much is added to recipes.

Strawberry Avocado Toast

SERVES 2

SERVING SIZE
1 toast

IMMUNE-BOOSTING FOODS: ③

My teenage girls are now old enough to make their own breakfast, and a favorite go-to is avocado toast. They have been experimenting with many toppings, and this combination of strawberries with a little extra crunch from sunflower seeds is one of their favorites.

1 avocado, sliced lengthwise and pitted

2 slices 100% whole wheat bread, toasted

4 strawberries, stems removed and sliced

2 tsp (10 mL) unsalted roasted sunflower seeds

Balsamic vinegar

$\frac{1}{8}$ tsp (0.5 mL) kosher salt

1 Spoon half an avocado onto each slice of toast and mash with a fork.

2 Top the avocado on each toast with 2 sliced strawberries and 1 tsp (5 mL) of the sunflower seeds. Drizzle each with $\frac{1}{8}$ tsp (0.5 mL) balsamic vinegar and sprinkle with the salt. Serve immediately.

> **TOBY'S TIP** When selecting ripe Hass avocados, the kind most commonly found in grocery stores, choose those with dark skin that slightly yield to gentle pressure.

Smoked Salmon Crostini

These crostini are certainly gorgeous, but the most beautiful thing is that they take less than 30 minutes to whip up. Make them as delicious and simple hors d'oeuvres to serve at any party, or try them as a creative snack for the family.

SERVING SIZE
4 pieces

IMMUNE-BOOSTING FOODS: ①

¾ baguette, preferably whole wheat

3 tbsp (45 mL) olive oil

¾ cup (175 mL) whipped cream cheese

2 tbsp (30 mL) chopped dill

⅛ tsp (0.5 mL) ground black pepper

¾ English cucumber, thinly sliced (48 pieces; see Note)

4 oz (125 g) smoked salmon, cut into 24 bite-size pieces

3 tbsp (45 mL) capers

PREHEAT THE OVEN TO 400°F (200°C)

1 Cut the baguette on a diagonal into twenty-four ¼-inch (0.5 cm) slices. Arrange them in an even layer on a baking sheet.

2 Brush the olive oil over both sides of the baguette slices. Bake, turning the slices over halfway through, until the bread is golden brown, about 8 minutes.

3 In a small bowl, combine the cream cheese, dill and black pepper, and mix well.

4 To assemble, spread about 1 tsp (5 mL) of the cream cheese mixture over each toasted baguette slice. Press 2 cucumber slices on the top of the cream cheese mixture and then place 1 piece of smoked salmon over the cucumbers. Garnish with 2 or 3 capers.

NOTE For very thin slices of cucumber, use a mandoline slicer.

TOBY'S TIPS

English cucumbers work well in appetizers like these because they have fewer seeds and are less watery than the regular slicer cucumbers typically found at grocery stores.

To minimize food waste, dip leftover cucumber slices in extra cream cheese mixture, hummus or your dressing of choice.

Sweet Potato Rounds WITH
GOAT CHEESE, PECANS AND CRANBERRIES

SERVES 6

SERVING SIZE
3 rounds

IMMUNE-
BOOSTING
FOODS: ①

Using sweet potatoes as the base for these bite-size snacks is a nice way to incorporate the immune-boosting ingredient into your day. These also make a great appetizer or game-day snack.

Baking sheet coated with cooking spray

2 sweet potatoes, sliced into eighteen ½-inch (1 cm) rounds (see Note)

2 tbsp (30 mL) olive oil

¼ tsp (1 mL) kosher salt

⅛ tsp (0.5 mL) ground black pepper

½ cup (125 mL) raw pecans, coarsely chopped

4 oz (125 g) chèvre (fresh goat cheese)

1 tbsp (15 mL) pure maple syrup

¼ tsp (1 mL) dried thyme

½ cup (125 mL) dried cranberries

PREHEAT THE OVEN TO 425°F (220°C)

1 In a large bowl, place the sweet potato rounds. Add the oil, salt and pepper. Toss to evenly coat the potatoes.

2 Place the sweet potato rounds in a single layer about ½ inch (1 cm) apart on the prepared baking sheet. Bake until slightly browned, 22 to 25 minutes, flipping halfway through. Remove the baking sheet from the oven and let the sweet potatoes cool for at least 10 minutes. Use a spatula to transfer the rounds to a serving plate.

3 While the sweet potatoes are in the oven, heat the pecans in a small skillet over medium-low heat, stirring occasionally, until slightly toasted, about 5 minutes. Transfer the toasted pecans to a clean bowl.

4 In a medium bowl, use the back of a fork to mash the goat cheese. Add the maple syrup and thyme and stir to combine.

5 On each round, spoon about 1 tsp (5 mL) of the cheese mixture and, using a butter knife, spread across the top of the sweet potato round. Top with about 1 tsp (5 mL) of the pecans and 1 tsp (5 mL) of the cranberries. Using clean fingers, gently push down on the toppings so they stick to the cheese mixture. Serve immediately.

NOTE
Use long, narrow sweet potatoes for even rounds. Be sure to thoroughly dry them after washing to allow them to brown.

TOBY'S TIP | Swap the cranberries for raisins, tart cherries or small pieces of dried fruit of your choice.

CHAPTER 6

SOUPS AND SANDWICHES

Hearty Lentil-Tomato Soup

This robust soup is brimming with good-for-you nutrients like filling fiber and the antioxidant vitamin C. It's also filled with the immune-boosting ingredients turmeric, ginger, garlic and lentils. Enjoy this warming soup with a slice of crusty bread.

SERVING SIZE
1¼ cup (300 mL)

IMMUNE-BOOSTING FOODS: ④

2 tbsp (30 mL) olive oil

1 yellow onion, chopped

4 cloves garlic, minced

3 stalks celery, chopped

2 carrots, shredded

1 tsp (5 mL) ground cumin

½ tsp (2 mL) ground turmeric

½ tsp (2 mL) ground ginger

⅛ tsp (0.5 mL) hot pepper flakes

3 cups (750 mL) tomato purée

3 cups (750 mL) low-sodium vegetable broth

1 cup (250 mL) water

1 cup (250 mL) dried red lentils

¾ tsp (3 mL) salt

¼ tsp (1 mL) ground black pepper

1 In a large pot, heat the olive oil over medium heat. When the oil is shimmering, add the onion and cook until translucent, about 3 minutes. Add the garlic and continue cooking until fragrant, an additional 30 seconds. Add the celery and carrots and continue cooking until softened, about 3 minutes. Add the cumin, turmeric, ginger and hot pepper flakes to the pot, and stir for 30 seconds. Add the tomato purée, vegetable broth, water and lentils, and bring to a boil over high heat.

2 When the mixture is boiling, reduce the heat to medium-low and simmer, covered, stirring occasionally, until lentils are soft and the flavors combine, about 40 minutes. Stir in the salt and black pepper.

3 Ladle 1¼ cup (300 mL) of soup into each of six soup bowls. Serve warm.

TOBY'S TIP | When cooking lentils, add the salt after cooking, otherwise the lentils can become tough.

TOBY'S TIPS | To dial down the kick, reduce the cayenne pepper to ⅛ tsp (0.5 mL) or leave it out entirely.

When prepping asparagus, discard the woody parts of the stalk.

To make this soup vegan, eliminate the Parmesan cheese or replace it with nutritional yeast.

Creamy Asparagus Soup

This lighter version of cream of asparagus soup is made with Yukon gold potatoes, which give it a silky-smooth texture without using heavy cream. Enjoy with a sandwich at lunch or as a starter soup at dinner.

SERVING SIZE
1²/₃ cups
(400 mL)

IMMUNE-
BOOSTING
FOODS: ②

Baking sheet lined with parchment paper

Immersion blender or blender

2 lbs (1 kg) asparagus, trimmed and cut into 1-inch (2.5 cm) pieces

3 tbsp (45 mL) olive oil

¾ tsp (3 mL) salt

1 leek (white and light green parts only), chopped

4 cloves garlic, minced

1 tsp (5 mL) dried thyme

1 tsp (5 mL) dried basil

1 tsp (5 mL) dried oregano

¼ tsp (1 mL) cayenne pepper

2 Yukon gold potatoes, peeled and cut into ½-inch (1 cm) cubes

2 cups (500 mL) low-sodium vegetable broth

1½ cups (375 mL) unsweetened almond milk

1 tbsp (15 mL) fresh lemon juice

8 tsp (40 mL) grated Parmesan cheese

PREHEAT THE OVEN TO 400°F (200°C)

1 In a large bowl, toss the asparagus with 1 tbsp (15 mL) of the oil and ¼ tsp (1 mL) of the salt until coated.

2 Arrange the asparagus on the prepared baking sheet in a single layer. Roast until the asparagus is slightly browned, 10 to 12 minutes, tossing halfway through. Remove the baking sheet from the oven and set aside to cool for 5 minutes.

3 In a large pot, heat the remaining 2 tbsp (30 mL) oil over medium heat. When the oil is shimmering, add the leek and cook until translucent, about 3 minutes. Add garlic and continue cooking until fragrant, 30 seconds. Add the thyme, basil, oregano, cayenne pepper and potatoes, and stir for 30 seconds. Stir in the asparagus, vegetable broth and almond milk and bring to a boil over high heat. Lower the heat to medium-low and simmer, covered, until the potatoes are fork-tender, about 20 minutes. Add the lemon juice and remaining ½ tsp (2 mL) salt and stir to combine. Remove the pot from the heat and let cool for 10 to 15 minutes until slightly cooled. Using an immersion blender or blender, pulse the soup until smooth and creamy, about 1 minute.

4 Ladle 1²/₃ cups (400 mL) of the soup into each of four soup bowls and sprinkle each with 2 tsp (10 mL) of the cheese.

Vegetable Beef Soup

SERVES 8

SERVING SIZE
1¹/₂ cups
(375 mL)

IMMUNE-
BOOSTING
FOODS: ②

This filling beef stew is brimming with ingredients to help boost your immune system. Beef and garlic are on the top 25 immune-boosting foods list, but the vegetables like tomatoes and potatoes are also sources of the antioxidant vitamin C, which contributes to a healthy immune system.

3 tbsp (45 mL) olive oil

1 lb (500 g) beef stew meat, cut into 1-inch (2.5 cm) pieces

1 yellow onion, chopped

2 cloves garlic, minced

2 carrots, peeled and chopped

2 stalks celery, chopped

4 cups (1 L) low-sodium beef broth

3 cups (750 mL) water

1 can (14 oz/398 mL) diced tomatoes, with juice

2 russet potatoes, peeled and cut into 1-inch (2.5 cm) cubes

1 tbsp (15 mL) dried Italian seasoning

¹/₂ tsp (2 mL) salt

¹/₄ tsp (1 mL) ground black pepper

1 cup (250 mL) frozen peas

1 cup (250 mL) frozen corn

1 cup (250 mL) frozen green beans

1 In a large pot, heat 1 tbsp (15 mL) of the oil over medium heat. When the oil is shimmering, add half the stew meat. Cook until browned on all sides, about 6 minutes. Remove the browned meat and place onto a clean plate. Heat another 1 tbsp (15 mL) of the oil in the same pot. Add the remaining stew meat and repeat the process.

2 Heat the remaining 1 tbsp (15 mL) oil in the pot. Add the onion, garlic, carrot and celery and cook until the vegetables have softened, about 5 minutes. Add the beef broth, water, tomatoes, potatoes, Italian seasoning, salt and black pepper. Stir to combine. Increase the heat to high and bring the mixture to a boil. Reduce the heat to low and simmer, covered, until the beef is cooked through and the potatoes are fork-tender, 20 minutes. Stir in the peas, corn and green beans and bring the mixture to a boil over high heat. Reduce the heat to medium-low and cook for 5 minutes.

3 Ladle 1¹/₂ cups of the soup into each of eight bowls. Serve warm.

TOBY'S TIP | When buying beef stew meat, the size of the meat is usually larger than 1 inch (2.5 cm) cubes. Cut the beef into smaller, bite-size pieces so they can fit nicely onto your soup spoon.

Ginger Chicken Soup

A cozy bowl of soup makes a great lunch. You can send it with your child to school or tote it to work in a thermos. Serve alongside the Avocado Egg Salad–Stuffed Pita (page 136) or Grilled Portobello Mushroom Caprese Sandwich (page 135).

SERVING SIZE
1¾ cups
(425 mL)

IMMUNE-
BOOSTING
FOODS: ②

1 tbsp (15 mL) olive oil

1 yellow onion, chopped

1 stalk celery, chopped

1 carrot, chopped

4 cloves garlic, minced

1 tbsp (15 mL) grated gingerroot

1 lb (500 g) boneless, skinless chicken thighs, fat trimmed and cut into 1-inch (2.5 cm) pieces

4 cups (1 L) low-sodium chicken broth

2 cups (500 mL) water

½ cup (125 mL) dry ditalini or orzo

Juice of ½ lemon

1 tbsp (15 mL) reduced-sodium soy sauce

2 cups (500 mL) chopped Lacinato kale, stems removed

1 In a large pot over medium heat, add the oil. When the oil is shimmering, add the onion, celery, carrot, garlic and ginger and cook until the vegetables soften, about 4 minutes. Add the chicken thighs and broth and bring to a boil over high heat. Reduce the heat to medium-low and simmer until the chicken is cooked, 15 minutes.

2 Add the water, ditalini or orzo, lemon juice and soy sauce and bring to a boil over high heat. Reduce the heat to medium-low and simmer, covered, until the flavors combine, about 20 minutes. Add the kale and cook, uncovered, until the kale wilts, about 5 minutes.

3 Ladle 1¾ cups (425 mL) of the soup into each of four bowls. Serve warm.

> **TOBY'S TIP**
> Swap the fresh ginger for 1 tsp (5 mL) ground ginger.
>
> Ditalini and orzo are small pastas perfect for soup. Feel free to use macaroni, rotini or any other pasta you would like.

Roasted Cauliflower Soup

Cauliflower's many healthy attributes include its ability to help boost your body's defense system. Although you may enjoy cauliflower raw or roasted, this creamy soup will make you fall in love with cauliflower all over again.

SERVING SIZE
1 1/2 cups
(375 mL)

IMMUNE-BOOSTING FOODS: ③

Baking sheet lined with parchment paper

Immersion blender or blender

2 medium heads cauliflower, cut into florets

3 tbsp (45 mL) olive oil

1 red onion, chopped

4 cloves garlic, minced

2 tsp (10 mL) ground cumin

1/2 tsp (2 mL) ground ginger

1/4 tsp (1 mL) smoked paprika

1/8 tsp (0.5 mL) ground nutmeg

1/8 tsp (0.5 mL) hot pepper flakes

3 cups (750 mL) low-sodium vegetable broth

1 cup (250 mL) unsweetened almond milk

Juice of 1/2 lemon

1/2 tsp (2 mL) salt

1/4 tsp (1 mL) ground black pepper

PREHEAT THE OVEN TO 425°F (220°C)

1 In a large bowl, toss the cauliflower with 2 tbsp (30 mL) of the oil to coat evenly. Arrange the cauliflower in single layer on the prepared baking sheet. Roast the cauliflower until it is browned, for about 25 minutes. Remove from the oven and set aside to cool slightly.

2 In a large pot, heat the remaining 1 tbsp (15 mL) oil over medium heat. When the oil is shimmering, add the onion and cook until translucent, about 3 minutes. Add in the garlic and continue cooking until fragrant, an additional 30 seconds. Add the cumin, ginger, smoked paprika, nutmeg and hot pepper flakes and continue to stir for 30 seconds. Add the cauliflower, vegetable broth, almond milk, lemon juice, salt and black pepper and bring to a boil over high heat. Reduce the heat to medium-low, cover and cook until the flavors combine, 15 minutes.

3 Remove the pot from the heat and set aside to cool for 15 minutes. Using an immersion blender or blender, purée the soup until smooth and creamy.

4 Ladle 1 1/2 cups (375 mL) of the soup into each of four bowls. Serve warm.

TOBY'S TIP | Always wait 15 to 20 minutes until a soup cools before putting in the blender. Placing very hot soup in a blender can cause a big mess as the soup tends to explode out of the blender!

Spiced Sweet Potato Soup

SERVES 6

SERVING SIZE
1⅓ cups
(325 mL)

IMMUNE-
BOOSTING
FOODS: ④

This soup is filled with aromatic warming spices, like ginger, turmeric, cinnamon and nutmeg. Don't forget to sprinkle on the pumpkin seeds before serving. Not only do they add a tasty crunch, but they also add immune-boosting antioxidants and zinc.

2 tbsp (30 mL) olive oil

1 sweet onion, chopped

1 tsp (5 mL) ground cumin

½ tsp (2 mL) grated fresh ginger

½ tsp (2 mL) ground turmeric

¼ tsp (1 mL) smoked paprika

¼ tsp (1 mL) cayenne pepper

¼ tsp (1 mL) ground cinnamon

¼ tsp (1 mL) ground nutmeg

2 lbs (1 kg) sweet potatoes (about 4), peeled and chopped

½ red apple, peeled and chopped

3 cups (750 mL) low-sodium vegetable broth

1 cup (250 mL) unsweetened coconut milk

Juice of 1 lemon

½ tsp (2 mL) salt

¼ tsp (1 mL) ground black pepper

2 tbsp (30 mL) unsalted pumpkin seeds

1 In a large pot, heat the olive oil over medium heat. When the oil is shimmering, add the onion and cook until soft and translucent, about 3 minutes. Add the cumin, ginger, turmeric, smoked paprika, cayenne pepper, cinnamon and nutmeg and stir for 1 minute. Add the sweet potatoes and apple, and stir to combine. Pour in the broth, coconut milk and lemon juice and bring to a boil over high heat. Reduce the heat to medium-low and cook, covered, stirring occasionally, until the sweet potatoes are fork-tender, 20 minutes. Stir in the salt and black pepper.

2 Let the soup cool for at least 10 minutes and pour into a blender or use an immersion blender to blend on High until smooth.

3 To serve, in each of eight bowls ladle 1⅓ cups (325 mL) of the soup and sprinkle each bowl with 1 tsp (5 mL) of pumpkin seeds.

> **TOBY'S TIP** | To ensure the recipe is gluten-free, check the label on the vegetable broth.

Smashed Chickpea and Sunflower Sandwich

SERVES 4

SERVING SIZE
1 sandwich

IMMUNE-
BOOSTING
FOODS: ②

The smashed chickpeas in this sandwich taste similar to hummus but are a little chunkier, and the sunflower seeds add a nice crunch. The fiber in the chickpeas and whole wheat bread combined with the healthy fat in the sunflower seeds help keep you feeling full longer.

2 cans (14 to 19 oz/398 to 540 mL) low-sodium chickpeas, drained and rinsed

½ cup (125 mL) raw sunflower seeds

¼ cup (60 mL) chopped red onion

¼ cup (60 mL) tahini

¼ cup (60 mL) fresh dill, chopped

Juice of 1 lemon

2 tsp (10 mL) Dijon mustard

1 tsp (5 mL) honey

8 slices 100% whole wheat bread, toasted

1 cup (250 mL) raw sprouts (such as alfalfa sprouts)

¼ English cucumber, thinly sliced

1 In a large bowl, mash the chickpeas using a fork or potato masher. Add the sunflower seeds, red onion, tahini, dill, lemon juice, mustard and honey and stir to incorporate.

2 Place 4 slices of the bread on each of four plates. Top each slice with about ¾ cup (175 mL) of the mash, ¼ cup (60 mL) of the sprouts and 4 or 5 slices of cucumber. Top with the second slice of whole wheat bread.

3 Cut in half and serve immediately.

> **TOBY'S TIP** | Swap the sprouts for arugula or lettuce.

Chipotle Chicken Sandwich
WITH AVOCADO

SERVES 4

SERVING SIZE
1 sandwich

IMMUNE-
BOOSTING
FOODS: ②

Do you ever crave a fast food sandwich, but don't want all that grease? This spiced chicken sandwich is the answer. Whip it up for a delicious lunch or dinner and your family will be begging for "at home" takeout from now on.

Grill pan or sauté pan coated with nonstick cooking spray

3 tbsp (45 mL) canola oil

Juice of 1 lime (about 1 tbsp or 15 mL)

2 tsp (10 mL) chipotle powder

2 tsp (10 mL) smoked paprika

2 tsp (10 mL) garlic powder

2 tsp (10 mL) cumin

2 tsp (10 mL) coriander

½ tsp (2 mL) salt

Four 5-oz (150 g) thinly sliced boneless skinless chicken breasts

1 avocado, peeled, pitted and thinly sliced

4 whole wheat rolls, toasted

¼ cup (60 mL) light mayonnaise

4 slices reduced-fat Monterey Jack cheese

1 tomato, thinly sliced

1 In a medium bowl, whisk together the canola oil, lime juice, chipotle powder, smoked paprika, garlic powder, cumin, coriander and salt. Add the chicken breasts and turn to coat. Cover the bowl and place in the refrigerator to marinate for at least 30 minutes and up to 24 hours.

2 Heat the prepared grill pan or sauté pan over medium heat. When the oil is shimmering, add the chicken and cook until the internal temperature reaches at least 165°F (74°C), 4 minutes on each side. Discard excess marinade.

3 Place several slices of avocado on one half of each roll and top with chipotle chicken. Spread 1 tbsp (15 mL) of the mayonnaise on the other half of each roll and top with 1 slice of cheese and 1 or 2 slices of tomato. Press the sandwiches together and enjoy.

> **TOBY'S TIPS** | To add spiciness, increase the chipotle powder and smoked paprika by 1 tsp (5 mL). Conversely, to decrease the spiciness, cut back on the two spices by 1 tsp (5 mL).

Salmon BLT

In my family the fights over what to eat for dinner are between salmon and bacon. One child wants salmon every night and the other would have bacon every meal of the day (if she could!). Instead of making separate dishes — I piled them all into one. Now that's a tasty compromise!

SERVING SIZE
1 sandwich

IMMUNE-BOOSTING FOODS: ①

Skillet coated with nonstick cooking spray

8 slices turkey bacon

Four 4-oz (125 g) salmon fillets

2 tsp (10 mL) Italian seasoning

¼ tsp (1 mL) salt

⅛ tsp (0.5 mL) ground black pepper

¼ cup (60 mL) light mayonnaise

1 tsp (5 mL) Thai chile sauce (such as Sriracha)

8 slices 100% whole wheat bread, toasted

1 plum (Roma) tomato, thinly sliced

4 leaves lettuce, halved

---

1 Heat the prepared skillet over medium-high heat. When the oil is shimmering, add the bacon and cook until crisp and brown, turning occasionally, about 6 minutes. Transfer the bacon to a paper towel–lined plate and let cool slightly. Wipe the skillet clean with a paper towel.

2 Sprinkle both sides of the salmon with the Italian seasoning, salt and black pepper.

3 Coat the same skillet with nonstick cooking spray and heat over medium heat. When the oil is shimmering, add the salmon fillets, skin-side down, and cook until the internal cooking temperature reaches 145°F (63°C), 10 minutes, turning once. Transfer the salmon to a clean plate.

4 In a small bowl, whisk together the mayonnaise and chile sauce.

5 Spread the chile-mayonnaise evenly onto each of 8 slices of toasted bread. Assemble the sandwiches by topping 4 slices of the bread with a few slices tomato, 2 pieces of lettuce, 2 slices of bacon and a salmon fillet. Place the second slice of bread on top and serve immediately.

> **TOBY'S TIPS**
>
> Opt for uncured bacon or turkey bacon whenever possible.
>
> If your salmon fillet is very thick, slice it on an angle and spread it out.

TOBY'S TIP

Make this sandwich into a panini! Skip step 4 and use your panini grill or "press" the sandwich on the same grill pan used for the mushrooms after the sandwiches are assembled. To use the grill pan, coat the pan with nonstick cooking spray and heat over medium-low heat. Place the sandwich onto the pan and press down with the clean bottom of a second pan until the cheese has slightly melted, about 3 minutes on each side.

Grilled Portobello Mushroom Caprese Sandwich

SERVES 4

SERVING SIZE
1 sandwich

IMMUNE-
BOOSTING
FOODS: ①

Filled with fresh mozzarella, tomatoes and basil, this traditional Italian sandwich is taken to the next level with an immune-boosting grilled mushroom. Flavored with tangy-sweet balsamic dressing, this sandwich is out of this world.

Grill pan or sauté pan coated with nonstick cooking spray

Panini grill (optional)

¼ cup (60 mL) balsamic vinegar

2 tsp (10 mL) Dijon mustard

1 tsp (5 mL) dried rosemary

½ tsp (2 mL) salt

½ cup (125 mL) olive oil

4 large portobello mushrooms, stems removed and discarded

4 ciabatta rolls, sliced open

12 fresh basil leaves

4 oz (125 g) fresh mozzarella cheese, cut into 4 slices

2 plum (Roma) tomatoes, thinly sliced

1 In a large bowl, whisk together the balsamic vinegar, mustard, rosemary and salt. Slowly drizzle in the oil, continuously whisking, until incorporated. Spoon 2 tbsp (30 mL) of the dressing into a small bowl or ramekin and set aside.

2 Add the mushroom caps to the large bowl with the marinade and turn to coat. Let marinate for 10 to 15 minutes.

3 Heat the prepared grill pan or sauté pan over medium heat. When the oil is shimmering, remove the mushrooms from the marinade and shake off excess. Add the mushrooms to the pan and cook until tender, 10 minutes, flipping once. Transfer the mushrooms to a clean plate. Discard the marinade from the mushrooms.

4 Coat the same pan with nonstick cooking spray and place over medium-low heat. Place the rolls cut-side down onto the pan and toast until golden, about 3 minutes on each side. Transfer the toasted rolls to a cutting board, cut-side up.

5 Evenly spoon the reserved marinade onto each roll half. Top each of 4 halves with 3 basil leaves, 1 slice mozzarella cheese, several tomato slices and a cooked portobello mushroom cap. Top the four sandwiches with the second roll half. Serve immediately.

Avocado Egg Salad–Stuffed Pita

SERVES 6

SERVING SIZE
1 sandwich

IMMUNE-
BOOSTING
FOODS: ②

Looking to up your egg salad game? Combine these two immune-boosting foods — avocados and eggs — to create a silky-smooth salad. The flavors meld so beautifully together!

6 large eggs

2 avocados, halved and pitted

2 tbsp (30 mL) light mayonnaise

2 tbsp (30 mL) nonfat plain Greek yogurt

2 tbsp (30 mL) chopped fresh dill

Juice of ½ lemon

¼ tsp (1 mL) salt

⅛ tsp (0.5 mL) ground black pepper

6 large whole wheat pitas

6 leaves lettuce, halved

2 plum (Roma) tomatoes, thinly sliced

1 In a medium pot, cover the eggs with water. Place the pot over high heat and bring the water to a boil. Boil the eggs for 3 minutes, then remove the pot from the heat, cover, and let the eggs stand for 15 minutes. Drain the water from the pot, and run cold water over the eggs until they are completely cool, about 10 minutes. Peel the eggs and coarsely chop.

2 Place the chopped eggs in a medium bowl. Using a spoon, scoop the avocados out of their skins and add to the eggs. Using the back of a fork or a potato masher, mash the egg and avocado mixture. Add the mayonnaise, yogurt, dill, lemon juice, salt and pepper and stir until combined.

3 Slice 1 inch (2.5 cm) from the top of the pitas to open them.

4 Stuff each of the pitas with an even amount of lettuce and tomatoes. Add about ½ cup (125 mL) of the egg mixture. Serve immediately.

TOBY'S TIP I typically call for plum (Roma) tomatoes in sandwiches, as they don't have many seeds and aren't as juicy as other tomatoes, which keeps the bread from getting soggy.

Roast Beef and Sautéed Onion Sandwich

SERVES 4

SERVING SIZE
1 sandwich

IMMUNE-
BOOSTING
FOODS: ①

Deli sandwiches are certainly an easy lunch, and this roast beef sandwich takes about 10 minutes total to whip up. The sautéed onions and melted cheese turn this everyday lunch into a home run your entire family will be cheering about.

1 tbsp (15 mL) olive oil

1 yellow onion, sliced lengthwise and cut into ½-inch (1 cm) half-moons

8 slices seedless 100% rye bread

8 tsp (40 mL) Dijon mustard

12 oz (375 g) low-sodium deli sliced roast beef

4 slices reduced-fat Cheddar cheese

Nonstick cooking spray

1 In a large skillet, heat the oil over medium heat. When the oil is shimmering, add the onion and cook until slightly softened, 5 minutes. Transfer the onion to a clean bowl. Use a paper towel to wipe the skillet clean.

2 Place the bread slices onto a cutting board. Spread 1 tsp (5 mL) of mustard onto each slice. Top each of 4 slices with 3 oz (90 g) of roast beef and 1 slice of cheese. Divide the onions evenly among the sandwiches and place on top of the cheese.

3 Coat the same skillet with the cooking spray and heat over medium heat. When the oil is shimmering, add one or two sandwiches at a time and cook for 3 to 4 minutes on each side, pressing down on the sandwich with the spatula. Transfer the cooked sandwiches to clean plates and repeat with the remaining sandwiches.

4 Slice each sandwich in half and serve immediately.

> **TOBY'S TIP** | There are many deli options for lighter roast beef, including all-natural grilled roast beef or top round roast beef. If you're unsure, ask the person behind the deli counter about healthier roast beef choices.

CHAPTER 7

SALADS

Spinach Salad
WITH STRAWBERRIES AND ALMONDS

SERVES 4

SERVING SIZE
1¼ cups (300 mL)
plus 2 tbsp
(30 mL) dressing

IMMUNE-
BOOSTING
FOODS: ③

Part of a healthy diet is taking in plenty of vegetables. However, only one in ten people get the recommended amount of vegetables each day. This go-to immune-boosting salad can be put together in about 15 minutes. Serve alongside a sandwich or soup, or as a starter for dinner.

DRESSING

2 tbsp (30 mL) red wine vinegar

4 tsp (20 mL) honey

2 tsp (10 mL) sesame seeds

2 tsp (10 mL) Dijon mustard

2 tsp (10 mL) fresh lemon juice

¼ tsp (1 mL) salt

⅛ tsp (0.5 mL) ground black pepper

¼ cup (60 mL) extra virgin olive oil

SALAD

¼ cup (60 mL) sliced almonds

4 cups (1 L) spinach, packed

1 cup (250 mL) strawberries, sliced

¼ cup (60 mL) crumbled feta cheese

1 TO MAKE THE DRESSING: In a small bowl, whisk together the vinegar, honey, sesame seeds, mustard, lemon juice, salt and pepper until well combined. While continuously whisking, add the oil until incorporated.

2 TO MAKE THE SALAD: In a small saucepan, heat the almonds over medium-low heat until toasted, about 5 minutes. Transfer the toasted almonds to a small bowl and let cool slightly.

3 In a large serving bowl, add the spinach and top with the strawberries, almonds and feta cheese. Drizzle the dressing on top of the salad before serving and toss lightly to combine.

> **TOBY'S TIPS**
>
> The dressing can be made up to 5 days in advance and stored in a sealed container in the refrigerator.
>
> When taking the salad to go, pack the dressing in a small, separate container on the side and pour on the salad right before eating.
>
> Swap the sliced almonds for unsalted dry roasted slivered almonds.

Pear Salad
WITH WALNUTS AND DRIED CRANBERRIES

SERVING SIZE
1 2/3 cups
(400 mL) plus
about 2 tbsp
(30 mL) dressing

IMMUNE-
BOOSTING
FOODS: ②

This side salad is perfect to pair with soup or a sandwich for lunch or to serve as a starter salad for dinner. If you want to make it a main salad, top with rotisserie chicken or leftover chicken breast.

VINAIGRETTE

½ cup (125 mL) balsamic vinegar

1 clove garlic, minced

2 tsp (10 mL) Dijon mustard

1 tsp (5 mL) onion powder

1 tsp (5 mL) granulated sugar

⅛ tsp (0.5 mL) salt

¼ cup (60 mL) extra virgin olive oil

SALAD

½ cup (125 mL) raw or dry roasted, unsalted walnuts, coarsely chopped

6 cups (1.5 L) mixed greens

1 pear, cored and thinly sliced into half-moons

¼ cup (60 mL) dried cranberries

¼ cup (60 mL) shaved Parmesan cheese

1 TO MAKE THE DRESSING: Whisk together the balsamic vinegar, garlic, mustard, onion powder, sugar and salt in a small bowl. While continually whisking, slowly drizzle in the olive oil until incorporated.

2 TO MAKE THE SALAD: Heat the walnuts in a small saucepan over medium-low heat. Cook, tossing regularly, until the walnuts are toasted, 5 minutes. Remove the walnuts from the pan and set aside to cool for at least 10 minutes.

3 In a large salad bowl, add the mixed greens and top with the sliced pear and cranberries. Sprinkle with the Parmesan cheese. Drizzle the dressing onto the salad right before serving.

> **TOBY'S TIPS**
>
> Swap the dried cranberries for dried cherries.
>
> To save time, prepare the balsamic vinaigrette up to 5 days ahead of time and store it in a sealed container in the refrigerator, or use a store-bought version.

Roasted Sweet Potato Salad
WITH AVOCADO

SERVES 6

SERVING SIZE
1½ cups
(375 mL)

**IMMUNE-
BOOSTING
FOODS:** ④

This salad provides a starch, vegetable, fat, and protein (from the seeds!). It's a nicely balanced salad that is perfect for lunch or as a side at dinner.

Baking sheet lined with aluminum foil and coated with nonstick cooking spray

DRESSING

¼ cup (60 mL) apple cider vinegar

1 tbsp (15 mL) pure maple syrup

Zest and juice of 1 lemon

¼ tsp (1 mL) salt

⅛ tsp (0.5 mL) ground black pepper

⅓ cup (75 mL) olive oil

SALAD

2 sweet potatoes, peeled and cut into ½-inch (1 cm) cubes

2 tbsp (30 mL) olive oil

¼ tsp (1 mL) salt

⅛ tsp (0.5 mL) ground black pepper

3 cups (750 mL) chopped Lacinato kale (see Note)

3 cups (750 mL) baby spinach, coarsely chopped

½ red onion, finely chopped

1 avocado, pitted, peeled and cut into slices

6 tbsp (90 mL) crumbled goat cheese

6 tbsp (90 mL) raw or unsalted dry roasted sunflower seeds

PREHEAT THE OVEN TO 425°F (220°C)

1 TO MAKE THE DRESSING: In a small bowl, whisk together the apple cider vinegar, maple syrup, lemon zest and juice, salt and pepper. While continuously whisking, slowly drizzle in the oil.

2 TO MAKE THE SALAD: In a medium bowl, add the sweet potatoes, oil, salt and pepper and toss to evenly coat. Place the sweet potatoes in a single layer on the prepared baking sheet. Cook until slightly browned, about 15 minutes, flipping once halfway through. Remove the baking sheet from the oven and let cool for at least 10 minutes.

3 In a large bowl, add the kale, spinach, onion and sweet potatoes. Add the dressing and toss to evenly coat.

NOTE
To prep the kale, remove hard stems before measuring. To reduce food waste, finely chop the stems and include them in the salad.

4 In each of six serving bowls, spoon $1\frac{1}{3}$ cups (325 mL) of the kale mixture and top with a few slices of avocado and 1 tbsp (15 mL) of the goat cheese and 1 tbsp (15 mL) of the sunflower seeds. Serve immediately.

> ### TOBY'S TIPS
>
> You can serve this salad family-style or meal prep and store in individual containers. If you choose to meal prep the salad, add the dressing right before eating.
>
> If you're looking to add more protein to this salad, add leftover grilled chicken breast or shred rotisserie chicken over it.

Orzo Salad
WITH RED BELL PEPPERS AND MOZZARELLA

Pasta salad is always a favorite, but did you know you can bulk it up with lots of veggies? Vegetables provide an array of immune-boosting nutrients including vitamins A and C (depending on the vegetable), plus they add texture and flavor.

6 oz (175 g) dry whole wheat orzo

5 tbsp (75 mL) olive oil

4 cups (1 L) baby spinach

1 cup (250 mL) fresh basil, coarsely chopped

2 tbsp (30 mL) red wine vinegar

2 cloves garlic, minced

$\frac{1}{4}$ tsp (1 mL) salt

$\frac{1}{8}$ tsp (0.5 mL) ground black pepper

1 red bell pepper, diced

4 oz (125 g) fresh mozzarella cheese, cut into $\frac{1}{2}$-inch (1 cm) cubes

1 cup (250 mL) grape tomatoes, halved

SERVES 6

SERVING SIZE
About $\frac{3}{4}$ cup (175 mL)

IMMUNE-BOOSTING FOODS: ③

1 Fill a medium saucepan three-quarters full with water and bring to a boil over high heat. Add the orzo and cook until al dente, 7 to 8 minutes. Drain the orzo and let cool for 10 minutes.

2 In a large skillet, heat 1 tbsp (15 mL) of the oil over medium heat. Add the spinach and basil and cook until wilted, 3 to 4 minutes. Remove from the heat and set aside to cool slightly.

3 In a small bowl, whisk together the vinegar, garlic, salt and black pepper. Slowly drizzle in the remaining $\frac{1}{4}$ cup (60 mL) oil, continuously whisking, until incorporated.

4 In a separate large bowl, add the orzo and spinach mixture and toss to combine. Add the bell pepper, cheese and tomatoes and toss to evenly incorporate. Drizzle the dressing onto the salad and toss to evenly coat.

5 Serve immediately or store in a covered container for up to 4 days in the refrigerator.

> **TOBY'S TIP** | Swap the orzo for macaroni or another smaller-size pasta.

Soba Noodle Salad
WITH ALMOND-GINGER DRESSING

SERVES 6

SERVING SIZE
1³/₄ cups
(425 mL)

IMMUNE-
BOOSTING
FOODS: ④

This dish combines grains, protein and vegetables to make a well-balanced dish. It's a perfect all-in-one meal to tote to work or eat while working from home.

8 oz (250 g) soba (buckwheat) noodles

1 cup (250 mL) frozen shelled edamame

¹/₃ cup (75 mL) water

3 tbsp (45 mL) creamy almond butter

3 tbsp (45 mL) reduced-sodium soy sauce or tamari

2 tbsp (30 mL) honey

Juice of 1 lime

1 tbsp (15 mL) unseasoned rice vinegar

¹/₂ tsp (2 mL) ground ginger

1 carrot, grated

1 red bell pepper, chopped

¹/₂ English cucumber, chopped

1 green onion (white and green parts), chopped

¹/₄ cup (60 mL) cilantro, chopped

6 tbsp (90 mL) unsalted dry roasted almonds, coarsely chopped

1 Fill a large pot three-quarters full with water and bring to a boil over high heat. Add the soba noodles and reduce the heat to medium. Boil until tender, 8 minutes. Add the edamame 3 minutes before the soba noodles are done cooking. Drain the soba noodles and edamame and run under cold water. Place in a large bowl and set aside to cool slightly.

2 In a small bowl, whisk the water, almond butter, soy sauce, honey, lime juice, rice vinegar and ginger. Add ¹/₂ cup (125 mL) of the almond-ginger dressing to the soba noodles. Toss evenly to coat.

3 In a medium bowl, add the carrot, bell pepper, green onion and cilantro and toss to combine.

4 Add the vegetable mixture to the soba noodles and edamame and toss to combine. Add the remaining dressing and toss to evenly coat.

5 To serve, place 1³/₄ cups (425 mL) of the salad onto each of six salad bowls. Sprinkle each with 1 tbsp (15 mL) of the chopped almonds. Serve immediately or cover and store in the refrigerator for up to 4 days.

> **TOBY'S TIP**
> This recipe is gluten-free if you use tamari. Just check the label to make sure your tamari is gluten-free.

Chopped Salad WITH SALMON

This Mediterranean-inspired chopped salad has a simple lemon and olive oil dressing. Add immune-boosting chickpeas and salmon and you've got a healthy, immune-friendly, delicious lunch or dinner.

Baking sheet coated with nonstick cooking spray

SALAD

4 cups (1 L) chopped romaine lettuce

1 can (14 to 19 oz/398 to 540 mL) low-sodium chickpeas, drained and rinsed

½ English cucumber, finely diced

2 plum tomatoes, finely diced

1 red bell pepper, finely diced

¼ cup (60 mL) fresh parsley, chopped

Juice of 1 lemon

2 tbsp (30 mL) extra virgin olive oil

¼ tsp (1 mL) salt

⅛ tsp (0.5 mL) ground black pepper

SALMON

1½ lbs (750 g) salmon fillet, cut into 4 equal pieces

⅛ tsp (0.5 mL) salt

⅛ tsp (0.5 mL) ground black pepper

2 lemons, thinly sliced

TO ASSEMBLE

¼ cup (60 mL) crumbled feta cheese

SERVES 4

SERVING SIZE
2 cups (500 mL) salad plus 6 oz (175 g) salmon

IMMUNE-BOOSTING FOODS: ③

PREHEAT THE OVEN TO 400°F (200°C)

1 TO MAKE THE SALAD: In a large bowl, add the lettuce, chickpeas, cucumber, tomatoes, bell pepper and parsley. Toss to combine. Add the lemon juice, oil, salt and black pepper and toss to evenly coat.

2 TO MAKE THE SALMON: Season both sides of the salmon with the salt and black pepper. Place skin-side down on the prepared baking sheet and arrange the lemon slices over the salmon. Bake until the fish is opaque and an instant-read thermometer inserted in the thickest part of a fillet registers 145°F (63°C), about 12 minutes. Remove the fish from the oven and let cool for 5 minutes.

3 TO ASSEMBLE: Divide the salad among four bowls and top with a salmon fillet. Sprinkle each equally with the feta cheese and serve.

> **TOBY'S TIPS** | To meal prep this dish, store the salad and fish separately in the refrigerator in sealable containers and eat within 3 days. Heat the fish in the microwave on High for 45 seconds and place over the salad.

Golden Cauliflower Salad

This creative salad is made by roasting cauliflower and tofu in a spice mixture and then tossing it with peppery arugula.

2 baking sheets lined with parchment paper

ROASTED CAULIFLOWER AND TOFU

3 tbsp (45 mL) olive oil

1 tbsp (15 mL) balsamic vinegar

3 cloves garlic, minced

1 tsp (5 mL) pure maple syrup

1 tsp (5 mL) ground cumin

1 tsp (5 mL) smoked paprika

1/2 tsp (2 mL) ground turmeric

1/4 tsp (1 mL) salt

1/8 tsp (0.5 mL) ground black pepper

1 head cauliflower, chopped into florets

1 lb (500 g) extra firm tofu, drained and diced into 1-inch (2.5 cm) cubes

DRESSING

3 tbsp (45 mL) tahini

3 tbsp (45 mL) nonfat plain Greek yogurt

2 tbsp (30 mL) water

2 tbsp (30 mL) olive oil

Juice of 1 lemon

1/2 tsp (2 mL) grated fresh ginger

1/8 tsp (0.5 mL) salt

1/8 tsp (0.5 mL) ground black pepper

TO ASSEMBLE

4 cups (1 L) arugula, packed

1/2 cup (125 mL) raw or unsalted dry roasted walnuts, coarsely chopped

PREHEAT THE OVEN TO 425°F (220°C)

1 TO MAKE THE ROASTED CAULIFLOWER AND TOFU: In a small bowl, whisk together the oil, vinegar, garlic, maple syrup, cumin, smoked paprika, turmeric, salt and black pepper.

2 In a large bowl, add the cauliflower and tofu. Pour the marinade over the cauliflower and tofu and toss to combine.

3 Arrange the cauliflower and tofu in a single layer on each of the prepared baking sheets. Roast until the cauliflower and tofu are browned, 25 to 30 minutes. Remove from the oven and let cool for 10 minutes.

4 TO MAKE THE DRESSING: In a small bowl, whisk together the tahini, Greek yogurt, water, olive oil, lemon juice, ginger, salt and black pepper.

5 TO ASSEMBLE: In a large bowl, toss together the arugula, cooled cauliflower and tofu, and sprinkle with the walnuts. Serve each salad with 1 tbsp (15 mL) of the tahini dressing on the side. Serve warm.

Cilantro-Lime Salad
WITH GRILLED CHICKEN AND AVOCADO

SERVES 6

SERVING SIZE
2 cups (500 mL)
salad plus 1 tbsp
(15 mL) dressing

IMMUNE-
BOOSTING
FOODS: ③

My family loves combining flavors inspired by Mexican cuisine, like cilantro, lime, black beans, corn, avocado and cheese. Although I can always order in from my favorite Mexican restaurant, making my own at home just makes me in control of the ingredients – and it just tastes so much fresher!

Grill pan or large skillet coated with nonstick cooking spray

CHICKEN

⅓ cup (75 mL) olive oil

Juice of 1 lime

2 tbsp (30 mL) fresh cilantro, chopped

1 tsp (5 mL) garlic powder

1 tsp (5 mL) ground cumin

¼ tsp (1 mL) salt

⅛ tsp (0.5 mL) ground black pepper

1 lb (500 g) thin-sliced boneless skinless chicken breasts, cut into 1-inch (2.5 cm) strips

DRESSING

¼ cup (60 mL) red wine vinegar

2 tsp (10 mL) honey

Juice of 1 lime

¼ tsp (1 mL) garlic powder

¼ tsp (1 mL) ground cumin

¼ tsp (1 mL) salt

⅛ tsp (0.5 mL) ground black pepper

⅓ cup (75 mL) olive oil

SALAD

4 cups (1 L) chopped romaine lettuce

1 cup (250 mL) fresh cilantro, chopped

1 cup (250 mL) grape tomatoes, halved

1 cup (250 mL) low-sodium canned black beans, drained and rinsed

1 cup (250 mL) low-sodium canned sweet corn kernels, drained and rinsed

1 red bell pepper, chopped

½ English cucumber, chopped

1 avocado, sliced lengthwise, pit removed and cubed

½ cup (125 mL) shredded reduced-fat Cheddar cheese

1 TO MAKE THE CHICKEN: In a small bowl, whisk together the oil, lime juice, cilantro, garlic powder, cumin, salt, and black pepper.

2 Place the chicken breasts in a large bowl and drizzle with the marinade. Turn to coat evenly. Cover and refrigerate for at least 30 minutes and up to 24 hours.

3 Heat the prepared grill pan or large skillet over medium heat. When the oil is shimmering, add the chicken and cook until the internal cooking temperature is 165°F (74°C), about 4 minutes on each side. Transfer the cooked chicken to a clean plate.

4 TO MAKE THE DRESSING: In a small bowl, whisk together the red wine vinegar, honey, lime juice, garlic powder, cumin, salt and black pepper. While continuously whisking, slowly drizzle in the oil until incorporated.

5 TO MAKE THE SALAD: In a large bowl, add the romaine, cilantro, tomatoes, black beans, corn, red bell pepper, and cucumber. Toss to combine. Drizzle with 6 tbsp (90 mL) of the dressing and toss to combine. Top with the chicken, avocado and cheese.

6 To serve, place 2 cups (500 mL) of the salad into each of six bowls. Serve immediately with the remaining dressing on the side.

> **TOBY'S TIP** | To meal prep this salad, store the dressing in a sealable container on the side and drizzle on right before eating.

Balsamic Steak Salad

This salad makes a healthy and filling lunch or dinner. Serve with a whole grain roll and you've got yourself a meal!

Grill pan or sauté pan coated with nonstick cooking spray

DRESSING

¼ cup (60 mL) balsamic vinegar

2 cloves garlic, minced

1 tsp (5 mL) onion powder

1 tsp (5 mL) honey

½ tsp (2 mL) dried rosemary

½ tsp (2 mL) salt

¼ tsp (1 mL) ground black pepper

¼ cup (60 mL) olive oil

SALAD

12 oz (375 g) beef tenderloin steak or top sirloin steak

½ English cucumber, sliced lengthwise and cut into ½-inch (1 cm) half-moons

1 cup (250 mL) cherry tomatoes, halved

6 radishes, halved lengthwise and thinly sliced into half-moons

¼ red onion, thinly sliced

5 oz (150 g) spring mix

1 avocado, pitted, peeled and thinly sliced

SERVES 4

SERVING SIZE
2½ cups
(625 mL) salad
plus 3 oz (90 g)
beef

IMMUNE-
BOOSTING
FOODS: ③

1 MAKE THE DRESSING: In a small bowl, whisk together the balsamic vinegar, garlic, onion powder, honey, rosemary, salt and pepper. While continuously whisking, slowly drizzle in the oil until incorporated.

2 MAKE THE SALAD: In a large bowl, add the steak and drizzle with ¼ cup (60 mL) of the dressing. Turn to coat the steak evenly. Cover and marinate in the refrigerator for at least 30 minutes and up to 24 hours.

3 Heat a grill pan or sauté pan over medium heat. When the oil is shimmering, add the steak and cook, covered, until an instant-read thermometer inserted in the thickest part registers 145°F (63°C), about 6 minutes on each side. Discard the marinade. Transfer the steak to a cutting board and let cool for 10 minutes, then slice against the grain into 1-inch (2.5 cm) pieces.

4 In a medium bowl, toss together the cucumber, tomatoes, radishes and red onion. In a large salad bowl, add the spring mix and top with the vegetable mixture and sliced avocado.

5 In each of four bowls, add 2½ cups (625 mL) of the spring mix and vegetables and top with 3 oz (90 g) of sliced steak. Drizzle each salad with about 1 tbsp (15 mL) of the dressing. Serve immediately.

TOBY'S TIP If you would like to meal prep this salad, store the dressing on the side and drizzle over the top right before eating.

Barbecue Chicken Cobb

This lighter version of a Cobb salad has the flavors you love with a zingy barbecue twist. Short on time? See Toby's Tips for a time-saving suggestion.

Blender

Grill pan or medium skillet coated with nonstick cooking spray

DRESSING

½ cup (125 mL) low-fat (1%) buttermilk

6 tbsp (90 mL) reduced-fat (2%) Greek yogurt

¼ cup (60 mL) light mayonnaise

2 tsp (10 mL) dried parsley flakes

1 tsp (5 mL) dried dill

1 tsp (5 mL) dried chives

½ tsp (2 mL) garlic powder

Juice of ½ lemon

½ tsp (2 mL) salt

⅛ tsp (0.5 mL) ground black pepper

⅛ tsp (0.5 mL) cayenne pepper

⅛ tsp (0.5 mL) smoked paprika

CHICKEN

6 tbsp (90 mL) ketchup

1 tbsp (15 mL) apple cider vinegar

2 tbsp (30 mL) Worcestershire sauce

1 tsp (5 mL) light brown sugar

1 tsp (5 mL) smoked paprika

1 clove garlic, minced

⅛ tsp (0.5 mL) salt

12 oz (375 g) boneless skinless chicken tenders

TO ASSEMBLE

4 cups (1 L) chopped romaine lettuce

2 large hard-boiled eggs, thinly sliced

2 plum (Roma) tomatoes, chopped

1 cup (250 mL) white button mushrooms, chopped

4 slices cooked nitrite-free turkey bacon, chopped

1 avocado, pitted, peeled and diced

1 TO MAKE THE DRESSING: Add the buttermilk, yogurt, mayonnaise, parsley, dill, chives, garlic powder, lemon juice, salt, black pepper, cayenne and smoked paprika to a blender and blend until smooth. Transfer to a sealable container and refrigerate for 20 minutes to allow the flavors to combine. The dressing can be kept in the refrigerator for up to 5 days.

2 TO MAKE THE CHICKEN: In a large bowl, whisk together the ketchup, apple cider vinegar, Worcestershire sauce, brown sugar, smoked paprika, garlic and salt. Add the chicken tenders and turn to coat evenly. Cover and refrigerate to marinate for at least 30 minutes and up to 24 hours.

3 Heat the prepared grill pan or medium skillet over medium heat. When the oil is shimmering, add the chicken, shaking off excess marinade, and cook until an instant-read thermometer inserted in the thickest part of a tender registers 165°F (74°C), about 5 minutes on each side. Discard excess marinade.

4 TO ASSEMBLE: On a large family-style serving platter or in a large bowl, arrange the lettuce. Over the lettuce, layer the eggs, tomatoes, mushrooms, bacon and avocado. Top with the chicken, then drizzle the dressing over the entire salad and serve immediately.

TOBY'S TIPS

To cut time on this recipe, opt for a light ranch bottled dressing.

If you choose to meal prep the salad, drizzle the dressing over the salad right before eating.

CHAPTER 8

MAINS

Lentil-Stuffed Eggplant

This nicely portioned main provides a healthy amount of plant-based protein from the lentils, and the canned tomatoes add more immune-boosting benefits with a boatload of the antioxidant vitamin C. Perfect for a meatless dinner any night of the week!

SERVING SIZE
1 eggplant half

IMMUNE-
BOOSTING
FOODS: ②

Baking sheet coated with cooking spray

Blender or food processor

2 eggplants, halved lengthwise

1/4 cup (60 mL) olive oil

Salt

1 yellow onion, chopped

1 carrot, chopped

2 cloves garlic, minced

1 can (14 to 19 oz/398 to 540 mL) low-sodium brown lentils, drained and rinsed

1 can (14 oz/398 mL) finely diced tomatoes, with juice

1 zucchini, grated

1/2 cup (125 mL) low-sodium vegetable broth

1 tsp (5 mL) dried parsley flakes

1/2 tsp (2 mL) smoked paprika

1/8 tsp (0.5 mL) ground black pepper

1/2 cup (125 mL) grated Parmesan cheese

1/4 cup (60 mL) panko bread crumbs, preferably whole wheat

PREHEAT THE OVEN TO 400°F (200°C)

1 Scoop out some of the flesh from the eggplant halves, leaving about 1 inch (2.5 cm) around the edge. Set the halves aside.

2 Add the scooped-out flesh and 1 tbsp (15 mL) of the oil to a blender or food processor and purée. Transfer the mixture to a clean bowl and set aside.

3 Brush both sides of the eggplant halves with 1 tbsp (15 mL) of the oil and place on the prepared baking sheet skin-side down. Sprinkle 1/4 tsp (1 mL) of the salt onto the flesh side of the eggplant halves. Bake until the eggplants are slightly softened and browned, 20 minutes.

4 Reduce the oven temperature to 350°F (180°C).

5 In a large skillet, heat the remaining 2 tbsp (30 mL) oil over medium heat. When the oil is shimmering, add the onion, carrot, and garlic and cook, stirring occasionally, until softened, 5 minutes. Add the puréed eggplant, lentils, tomatoes with juice, zucchini, vegetable broth, parsley, paprika, black pepper and 1/4 tsp (1 mL) salt and stir to combine. Increase the heat to high and bring the mixture to a boil. Reduce the heat to medium-low and simmer, stirring occasionally, until the flavors combine, 10 minutes. Remove the skillet from the heat and let cool for 10 minutes.

6 In a small bowl, mix the Parmesan cheese with the panko bread crumbs.

7 Divide the lentil mixture equally between each of the 4 eggplant halves. Top each eggplant half with 3 tbsp (45 mL) of the cheese-panko mixture. Return to the oven and bake until the cheese has melted and the top is slightly browned, 10 minutes. Remove from the oven and let the eggplant cool for 10 minutes.

8 On each of four plates, place 1 eggplant half. Serve warm.

> **TOBY'S TIP** | To make this dish gluten-free, use gluten-free panko. To make this dish vegan, swap nutritional yeast for the Parmesan cheese.

TOBY'S
TIP

Swap the sweet potato mash for traditional mashed potatoes.

Lentil Shepherd's Pie

This Irish dish is traditionally made with lamb or mutton and topped with mashed potatoes. In this vegetarian version, the filling is made with immune-boosting lentils and mushrooms and topped with even more immune-boosting power of sweet potatoes. Not only is it delicious, but it also helps keep your immune system in tip-top shape.

SERVING SIZE
1⅓ cup
(325 mL)

IMMUNE-BOOSTING FOODS: ④

13- by 9-inch (33 by 23 cm) glass baking dish coated with cooking spray

2 tbsp (30 mL) olive oil

1 yellow onion, chopped

1 carrot, chopped

1 stalk celery, chopped

2 cloves garlic, minced

8 oz (250 g) brown mushrooms, chopped

1 can (14 to 19 oz/398 to 540 mL) low-sodium brown lentils, drained and rinsed

2 tbsp (30 mL) all-purpose flour

3 cups (750 mL) low-sodium vegetable broth

¼ cup (60 mL) red wine

3 tbsp (45 mL) tomato paste

1 tsp (5 mL) dried parsley flakes

½ tsp (2 mL) dried thyme

½ tsp (2 mL) dried rosemary

½ cup (125 mL) frozen peas

¼ tsp (1 mL) salt

¼ tsp (1 mL) ground black pepper

4½ cups (1.125 mL) Sweet Potato Mash (page 224; see Note)

PREHEAT THE OVEN TO 350°F (180°C)

1 In a large sauté pan, heat the oil over medium heat. When the oil is shimmering, add the onion, carrot, celery and garlic and cook until softened, about 5 minutes. Add the mushrooms and cook until softened, 8 minutes. Add the brown lentils and stir to combine.

2 Sprinkle the flour over the lentil mixture and cook, stirring, for 1 minute. Add the broth, red wine, tomato paste, parsley, thyme, rosemary and peas; stir to combine. Increase the heat to high and bring the mixture to a boil. Reduce the heat to medium-low and simmer for 10 minutes, stirring occasionally. Add the salt and pepper and stir to combine.

3 Remove the sauté pan from the heat and let cool for 5 minutes before transferring the mixture to the prepared baking dish.

4 Spread the sweet potato mash evenly over the lentil mixture and sprinkle with the pecans. Bake until heated through, about 20 minutes.

5 Remove the dish from the oven and let cool for 10 minutes.

6 Divide the shepherd's pie among six dishes. Serve immediately.

NOTE
This uses one batch of Sweet Potato Mash. When preparing it for this dish, reserve the pecans for the top.

Chickpea and White Bean Burgers

SERVING SIZE
1 burger

IMMUNE-
BOOSTING
FOODS: ⑦

In this bean-based veggie burger, there are a whopping seven immune-boosting foods. Plus, the recipe uses ingredients that are easy to find and might just be in your pantry right now. It's a win-win all around!

Food processor or blender

Baking sheet coated with nonstick cooking spray

½ cup (125 mL) short-grain brown rice

1 cup (250 mL) low-sodium vegetable broth

2 tbsp (30 mL) olive oil or canola oil

1 yellow onion, chopped

1 red bell pepper, chopped

2 cloves garlic, minced

½ cup (125 mL) raw walnuts, coarsely chopped

½ cup (125 mL) gluten-free quick-cooking rolled oats

1 can (14 to 19 oz/398 to 540 mL) low-sodium chickpeas, drained and rinsed

1 can (14 to 19 oz/398 to 540 mL) low-sodium cannellini beans, drained and rinsed

2 tsp (10 mL) Italian seasoning

1 tsp (5 mL) lemon zest

1 tsp (5 mL) sriracha

½ tsp (2 mL) salt

⅛ tsp (0.5 mL) ground black pepper

1 large egg, beaten

1 ripe avocado, pitted, peeled and sliced

8 burger buns, preferably whole wheat

8 leaves lettuce, halved

1 tomato, thinly sliced

1 In a medium saucepan, heat the rice and vegetable broth over high heat and bring to a boil. Reduce the heat to low and simmer, covered, until the rice is cooked, 45 minutes. Remove the saucepan from the heat and let cool for at least 10 minutes. Fluff with a fork.

2 Preheat the oven to 375°F (190°C).

3 In a medium skillet, heat the oil over medium heat. When the oil is shimmering, add the onion, bell pepper and garlic and cook until the onion softens, 3 minutes. Remove the skillet from the heat and let the mixture cool for at least 10 minutes.

4 Into the bowl of a food processor or blender, add the walnuts and pulse until it reaches a flour-like consistency, 1 minute. Add the oats and pulse two or three times to combine.

5 In a large bowl, add the chickpeas and cannellini beans and use a potato masher or fork to mash until almost smooth. Add the cooled rice, onion mixture, Italian seasoning, lemon zest, sriracha, salt and black pepper and stir with a spoon to combine. Add the egg and stir to incorporate. Add the oat mixture and stir to combine.

6 Scoop $1/2$ cup (125 mL) of the mixture and, using clean hands, shape into a ball. Place the ball on the prepared baking sheet and flatten with your palm. Repeat to make a total of eight burger patties, leaving 1 inch (2.5 cm) between each. Bake for 30 minutes, flipping the patties once halfway through. Transfer the patties to a clean plate and let cool for 10 minutes.

7 While the patties are cooling, in a small bowl, add the avocado and mash using a potato masher or fork. Spread about 1 tbsp (15 mL) of the mashed avocado onto one half of each of the 8 buns. Top each with a patty and divide the lettuce and tomato slices evenly among the burgers. Serve immediately.

TOBY'S TIP | Enjoy a bunless burger served over a bed of greens.

TOBY'S TIP | Swap the cannellini beans for garbanzo beans.

Garlic and White Bean–Stuffed Mushrooms

SERVES 4

SERVING SIZE
1 mushroom

IMMUNE-
BOOSTING
FOODS: ③

Because of their umami, or savory, flavor, portobello mushrooms are often used as a substitute for meat, but unlike meat, they don't contain much protein. The beans in this vegetarian dish help balance the plate by providing starch, fiber and protein.

Baking sheet lined with parchment paper

Food processor or blender

MUSHROOMS

4 portobello mushroom caps, rinsed and dried well

1 tbsp (15 mL) olive oil

¼ tsp (1 mL) salt

⅛ tsp (0.5 mL) ground black pepper

STUFFING

1 can (14 to 19 oz/398 to 540 mL) reduced-sodium cannellini beans, rinsed and drained

2 garlic cloves, crushed

2 tbsp (30 mL) chopped flat-leaf parsley

1 tbsp (15 mL) fresh lemon juice

1 tbsp (15 mL) olive oil

½ tsp (2 mL) dried thyme

½ tsp (2 mL) dried oregano

¼ tsp (1 mL) salt

⅛ tsp (0.5mL) ground black pepper

TOPPING

2 tbsp (30 mL) walnuts, chopped

2 tbsp (30 mL) grated Parmesan cheese

PREHEAT THE OVEN TO 400°F (200°C)

1 TO MAKE THE MUSHROOMS: Place the mushroom caps stem-side down on the prepared baking sheet 1 inch (2.5 cm) apart. Drizzle with the oil and sprinkle with the salt and pepper. Bake until the mushrooms have softened, 8 minutes. Remove from the oven and let cool for 5 minutes. Turn the mushrooms over, stem-side up.

2 Reduce the oven temperature to 350°F (180°C).

3 TO MAKE THE STUFFING: In the bowl of a food processor or blender, add the beans, garlic, parsley, lemon juice, oil, thyme, oregano, salt and black pepper, and pulse until a rough paste forms, about 45 seconds.

4 TO MAKE THE TOPPING: In a small bowl, mix together the walnuts and Parmesan to form a crumble topping.

5 TO ASSEMBLE: Divide the stuffing equally among the mushroom caps and, using the back of a spoon, spread the stuffing evenly over the top of the mushroom. Top each mushroom with about 1 tbsp (15 mL) of the topping. Bake until the stuffing is warmed through and the topping has turned golden brown, about 10 minutes. Serve warm.

Whole Roasted Cauliflower
WITH TOMATO-PEPPER RAGU

SERVING SIZE
1 cauliflower
wedge plus
about 1 cup
(250 mL) ragu

IMMUNE-
BOOSTING
FOODS: ③

This recipe makes cauliflower the main attraction, served in an immune-boosting sauce brimming with the antioxidant vitamin C. It's also a perfect dish to meal prep to heat and eat when working at home or in the office.

11- by 9-inch (33 by 23 cm) glass baking dish coated with cooking spray

Food processor or blender

CAULIFLOWER

¼ cup (60 mL) olive oil

4 cloves garlic, minced

2 tsp (10 mL) Italian seasoning

¼ tsp (1 mL) salt

⅛ tsp (0.5 mL) ground black pepper

1 head cauliflower, outer leaves removed and stem trimmed flat, keeping the head intact

RAGU

4 oz (125 g) roasted red bell peppers, drained

2 tbsp (30 mL) olive oil or canola oil

1 shallot, chopped

1 carrot, chopped

1 stalk celery, chopped

3 cloves garlic, minced

½ cup (125 mL) white cooking wine or dry white wine

1 can (28 oz /796 mL) whole peeled tomatoes with juice

1 tsp (5 mL) honey

1 tsp (5 mL) dried parsley

1 tsp (5 mL) dried oregano

3 bay leaves

¼ tsp (1 mL) salt

⅛ tsp (0.5 mL) ground black pepper

PREHEAT THE OVEN TO 400°F (200°C)

1 TO MAKE THE CAULIFLOWER: In a small bowl, whisk together the olive oil, garlic, Italian seasoning, salt and black pepper.

2 Place the cauliflower head in the prepared baking dish and drizzle with the oil mixture. Using clean hands, rub it over the entire cauliflower head, including the bottom. Cover loosely with aluminum foil and bake until tender, 35 to 40 minutes. Remove the baking dish from the oven and let cool at least 10 minutes. Transfer to a cutting board and cut into four equal wedges.

3 TO MAKE THE RAGU: Add the roasted peppers to a food processor or blender and purée until smooth.

4 In a large sauté pan, heat the olive or canola oil over medium heat. When the oil is shimmering, add the shallot, carrot, celery and garlic and cook until the vegetables soften, about 5 minutes. Stir in the puréed roasted peppers, wine, tomatoes, honey, parsley, oregano, bay leaves, salt and black pepper. Using the back of the mixing spoon, break the tomatoes into smaller pieces. Raise the heat to high and bring the mixture to a boil. Reduce the heat to medium-low and simmer, covered, until the flavors combine, about 20 minutes. Remove the bay leaves from the ragu and discard.

5 To serve, place one piece of cauliflower into each of four soup bowls. Spoon about 1 cup (250 mL) of the ragu over the cauliflower. Serve warm.

> **TOBY'S TIP** | For the whole tomatoes in the ragu, you can swap in the same amount of diced tomatoes with the juice.

Chickpea Stew

This stew is my favorite type of dish—the kind where all you do is throw everything into one pot and let the stove do the rest of the work. It's also perfect if you'd like leftovers for lunch.

RICE

1½ cups (375 mL) long-grain brown rice

3 cups (750 mL) low-sodium vegetable broth

STEW

2 tbsp (30 mL) olive oil

1 yellow onion, chopped

3 cloves garlic, finely chopped

2 tbsp (30 mL) tomato paste

2 tsp (10 mL) dark brown sugar

1 tsp (5 mL) smoked paprika

1 tsp (5 mL) ground cumin

1 tsp (5 mL) dried parsley

½ tsp (2 mL) dried oregano

¼ tsp (1 mL) cayenne pepper

1 red bell pepper, chopped

2 carrots, chopped

1 russet potato, peeled and cut into 1-inch (2.5 cm) cubes

2 cans (14 to 19 oz/398 to 540 mL) low-sodium chickpeas, rinsed and drained

2 cups (500 mL) tomato purée

2 cups (500 mL) low-sodium vegetable broth

2 cups (500mL) packed baby spinach

¼ tsp (1 mL) salt

⅛ tsp (0.5 mL) ground black pepper

¼ cup (60 mL) fresh parsley, chopped

1 TO MAKE THE RICE: In a medium saucepan, add the rice and vegetable broth and bring to a boil over high heat. Reduce the heat to low and simmer, covered, until the rice is tender, 35 to 40 minutes. Transfer the rice to a clean bowl and cover with aluminum foil to keep warm.

2 TO MAKE THE STEW: In a large pot, heat the oil over medium heat. When the oil is shimmering, add the onion and cook until soft and translucent, about 3 minutes. Add the garlic and cook until fragrant, 30 seconds. Add the tomato paste, brown sugar, smoked paprika, cumin, dried parsley, oregano and cayenne pepper and stir for 1 minute. Add the bell pepper, carrots, potato and chickpeas. Toss to coat and cook for 1 minute more. Add the tomato purée and vegetable broth and bring to a boil over high heat. Reduce the heat to medium-low and cook, covered, until the potatoes are cooked through and the flavors combine, about 25 minutes. Stir in the spinach, salt and black pepper and cook until the spinach is wilted, 2 minutes.

3 To serve, divide the rice and stew among six bowls. Sprinkle with the chopped parsley. Serve warm.

Almond Crusted Snapper

Nut crusted fish is often available in the prepared section of my market, but it costs much more than making it myself! With this Almond Crusted Snapper, you can have a tasty dinner on the table in under 30 minutes from start to finish.

Baking sheet coated with nonstick cooking spray

Food processor

1 cup (250 mL) raw unsalted almonds, roughly chopped

½ cup (125 mL) parsley, roughly chopped

¼ cup (60 mL) olive oil

4 cloves garlic, crushed

2 tsp (10 mL) Dijon mustard

Salt

Ground black pepper

1½ lbs (750 g) red snapper, cut into 4 fillets

PREHEAT THE OVEN TO 375°F (190°F)

1 In a small skillet, heat the almonds over medium-low heat and cook for about 5 minutes until toasted. Transfer the almonds to a clean bowl and let cool for 5 minutes.

2 Add the cooled almonds to a food processor and pulse until it reaches a flour-like consistency. Add the parsley, olive oil, garlic, mustard, ⅛ tsp (0.5 mL) salt and ⅛ tsp (0.5 mL) pepper and pulse until a paste forms.

3 Place the snapper fillets skin-side down onto the prepared baking sheet. Sprinkle ⅛ tsp (0.5 mL) salt and ⅛ tsp (0.5 mL) pepper over the snapper. Divide the almond paste equally among the fillets and, using clean hands, gently press to spread over the tops.

4 Bake until an instant-read thermometer inserted in the thickest part of a fillet registers 145°F (63°C) and the snapper easily flakes with a fork, about 12 minutes. Serve warm.

TOBY'S TIPS

Substitute the snapper for any flaky white fish like grouper, pollack or tilapia.

To freeze, place each fillet into individual freezer-friendly sealable containers for up to 2 months. To thaw, place in the refrigerator overnight. To reheat, cook in a preheated oven at 350°F (180°C) until an instant-read thermometer inserted in the thickest part of a fillet registers 165°F (74°C), about 10 minutes. Alternatively, reheat in the microwave in a microwave-safe dish on High for 30 to 45 seconds.

Sheet Pan Salmon
WITH ASPARAGUS

When it comes to cooking, my motto is "easy to cook and easy to clean." This recipes takes less than 30 minutes to whip up and as with any sheet pan dinner, there are minimal dishes to clean. As for taste, my three kids devour this dish within minutes of it coming out of the oven.

Baking sheet lined with aluminum foil and coated with nonstick cooking spray

3 tbsp (45 mL) unsalted butter, softened

Olive oil

1 shallot, finely chopped (about $1/2$ cup/125 mL)

3 cloves garlic, minced

2 tbsp (30 mL) chopped parsley

2 tbsp (30 mL) chopped rosemary

$1/4$ tsp (1 mL) kosher salt

$1/8$ tsp (0.5 mL) ground black pepper

$1 1/2$ lbs (750 g) salmon fillet

1 bunch asparagus (about 2 lbs/1kg), trimmed

1 lemon, thinly sliced

PREHEAT THE OVEN TO 450°F (230°C)

1 In a small bowl, use a fork or potato masher to mash the softened butter. Add 1 tbsp (15 mL) olive oil, the shallot, garlic, parsley, rosemary, salt and pepper and stir to combine.

2 Place the salmon fillet, skin-side down, in the center of the prepared baking sheet. Spread half the butter mixture over the salmon.

3 Divide the asparagus and place on all sides of the fillet in a single layer. Drizzle 1 tbsp (15 mL) olive oil over the asparagus and place the lemon slices over the asparagus and salmon. Dollop the remaining butter in several places over the asparagus. Bake until an instant-read thermometer inserted in the thickest part of the fillet registers 145°F (63°C), 10 to 12 minutes.

4 To serve, divide the salmon into four equal fillets and place on four plates. Divide the asparagus among the plates and serve warm.

TOBY'S TIPS Use $1/2$ cup (125 mL) finely chopped yellow onion in place of the shallot.
Swap the herbs for anything in your refrigerator, like dill or thyme.

Garlic Shrimp WITH CHICKPEAS

Crunchy toasted chickpeas combined with mouthwatering shrimp get all your taste buds moving in this easy meal. Low-calorie shrimp takes no time to cook on a baking sheet.

Baking sheet coated with cooking spray

SHRIMP

2 tbsp (30 mL) olive oil

4 cloves garlic, minced

Zest and juice of 1 lemon

1 tsp (5 mL) sriracha

1 tsp (5 mL) dried parsley

1/4 tsp (1 mL) salt

1/8 tsp (0.5 mL) ground black pepper

1 1/2 lbs (750 g) large shrimp, peeled, deveined and tails removed

CHICKPEAS

2 cans (14 to 19 oz/398 to 540 mL) low-sodium chickpeas, drained and rinsed

2 tbsp (30 mL) olive oil

1/4 tsp (1 mL) salt

1/8 tsp (0.5 mL) ground black pepper

TO ASSEMBLE

1 lemon, thinly sliced

SERVING SIZE
1 3/4 cups
(425 mL)

IMMUNE-BOOSTING FOODS: ②

PREHEAT THE OVEN TO 450°F (230°C)

1 TO MARINATE THE SHRIMP: In a large bowl, whisk together the oil, garlic, lemon zest and juice, sriracha, parsley, salt and pepper. Add the shrimp and toss to evenly coat. Cover and refrigerate for 20 to 30 minutes.

2 TO MAKE THE CHICKPEAS: In a large bowl, add the chickpeas, oil, salt and pepper and stir to coat. Transfer to the prepared baking sheet in a single layer. Bake until golden, 15 to 20 minutes, tossing halfway through.

3 TO ASSEMBLE AND BAKE: Remove the shrimp from the marinade and place in a single layer over the chickpeas. Discard the marinade. Top the shrimp with the lemon slices. Bake until the shrimp is opaque and an instant-read thermometer inserted in a couple of shrimp registers 145°F (63°C), about 8 minutes. Remove the baking sheet and let cool for 10 minutes.

4 Divide the shrimp and chickpeas among four bowls and serve warm.

TOBY'S TIP | Try serving over orzo or spaghetti.

Cod WITH STRAWBERRY SALSA

SERVES 4

This simple recipe cooks up a mild white fish and tops it with a burst of flavor. It's a really fun combination of sweet and savory and an exciting way to get both fruits and vegetables into your meal.

SERVING SIZE
5 oz (150 g)
fish plus ½ cup
(125 mL) salsa

IMMUNE-
BOOSTING
FOODS: ①

SALSA

2 cups (500 mL) strawberries, stems removed and finely diced

1 jalapeño, stem and seeds removed, finely diced

¼ red onion, finely diced

¼ cup (60 mL) fresh cilantro, finely chopped

¼ cup (60 mL) fresh basil leaves, finely chopped

Juice of 1 lime

2 tbsp (30 mL) olive oil

⅛ tsp (0.5 mL) salt

COD

Four 5 oz (150 g) cod fillets

¼ tsp (1 mL) salt

⅛ tsp (0.5 mL) ground black pepper

2 tbsp (30 mL) olive oil

1 TO MAKE THE SALSA: In a medium bowl, add the strawberries, jalapeño, onion, cilantro and basil and toss to combine. Add the lime juice, oil and salt and toss to evenly coat.

2 TO MAKE THE COD: Sprinkle both sides of the cod fillets with the salt and black pepper.

3 In a large skillet, heat 1 tbsp (15 mL) of the oil over medium heat. When the oil is shimmering, add 2 of the cod fillets and cook until the internal temperature of the fish is 145°F (63°C), about 3 minutes on each side. Remove the fillets and place on a clean plate and cover with aluminum foil to keep warm. Heat the remaining 1 tbsp (15 mL) oil and repeat with the remaining 2 cod fillets.

4 To serve, place 1 cod fillet onto each of four dinner plates. Top with ½ cup (125 mL) of the salsa. Serve immediately.

> **TOBY'S TIP** | Good substitutes for cod are black cod, mahi mahi, sea bass or whiting.

Halibut Marsala

Often served with chicken, this immune-boosting mushroom sauce is also lovely over white fish. Halibut is full of B-vitamins and zinc, which is a mineral that plays a central role in keeping your immune system working properly.

SERVING SIZE
6 oz (175 g)
fish plus ¹/₂ cup
(125 mL) sauce

IMMUNE-
BOOSTING
FOODS: ①

Baking sheet coated with nonstick cooking spray

Four 6-oz (175 g) halibut fillets

Salt

Ground black pepper

2 tbsp (30 mL) olive oil

1 lb (500 g) mushrooms, thinly sliced

¹/₂ cup (125 mL) Marsala wine

¹/₂ cup (125 mL) low-sodium vegetable broth

¹/₄ cup (60 mL) cool water

2 tbsp (30 mL) unbleached all-purpose flour

PREHEAT THE OVEN TO 375°F (190°C)

1 Season the flesh side of the fish with ¹/₄ tsp (1 mL) salt and ¹/₈ tsp (0.5 mL) pepper. Place the fillets on the prepared baking sheet 1 inch (2.5 cm) apart. Bake until an instant-read thermometer inserted in the thickest part of a fillet registers 145°F (63°C), 12 to 15 minutes. Remove the fish from the oven and let cool for at least 10 minutes.

2 In a large skillet, heat the oil over medium heat. When the oil is shimmering, add the mushrooms and cook until softened, 8 minutes. Add the wine and broth and bring the mixture to a boil over high heat. Reduce the heat to medium and cook, stirring occasionally, for 5 minutes.

3 In a small bowl, whisk the water with the flour. Add the flour mixture into the skillet and continue whisking until the mixture thickens, about 2 minutes.

4 Add ¹/₄ tsp (1 mL) salt and ¹/₈ tsp (0.5 mL) pepper to the sauce and stir to combine.

5 Divide the fillets among four plates and top with Marsala sauce. Serve warm.

TOBY'S TIPS

You can find Marsala wine in the vinegar aisle in your supermarket next to other cooking wines like sherry and red and white cooking wines. Alternatively, you can check next to the marinades.

You can always swap the halibut for another white fish or thinly sliced chicken breasts.

Branzino WITH TOMATO, OLIVE AND GARLIC SAUCE

A mild white fish, branzino is quick and easy to cook. This light tomato and olive sauce paired with a splash of white wine and lemon juice complement the flavors beautifully.

2 tbsp (30 mL) olive oil

1 shallot, chopped

4 cloves garlic, minced

3 cups (750 mL) grape tomatoes, halved lengthwise

½ cup (125 mL) pitted Kalamata olives, halved lengthwise

2 tbsp (30 mL) white cooking wine or dry white wine

Juice of 1 lemon

1 tsp (5 mL) dried parsley flakes

½ tsp (2 mL) dried oregano

⅛ tsp (0.5 mL) hot pepper flakes

¼ tsp (1 mL) ground black pepper

Four 5-oz (150 g) branzino fillets, dried with a paper towel

¼ tsp (1 mL) salt

2 tbsp (30 mL) unsalted butter

1 In a large skillet, heat the oil over medium heat. When the oil is shimmering, add the shallot and garlic and cook until softened and fragrant, 2 minutes. Add the tomatoes and olives and cook until the tomatoes begin to soften, 5 minutes. Add the wine, lemon juice, parsley, oregano, hot pepper flakes and ⅛ tsp (0.5 mL) of the black pepper and stir to combine. Raise the heat to high and bring the mixture to a boil. Reduce the heat to medium-low and cook until reduced by half, about 5 minutes. Transfer to a clean bowl and cover to keep warm. Wipe out the skillet with a paper towel.

2 Sprinkle the flesh side of the branzino fillets with the salt and remaining ⅛ tsp (0.5 mL) black pepper.

3 In the same large skillet, heat 1 tbsp (15 mL) of the butter over medium heat. When shimmering, add 2 fillets skin-side down and cook for 3 minutes. Using a spatula, flip and cook until an instant-read thermometer inserted in the thickest part of a fillet registers 145°F (63°C), about 2 minutes more. Transfer to a clean plate and cover to keep warm. Repeat for the remaining 2 fillets.

4 Divide the fillets among four plates and top with the sauce. Serve warm.

> **TOBY'S TIP** | Many fish markets sell branzino whole. Ask your local fishmonger to fillet two whole branzino fish for you.

Pasta WITH CHICKEN, SPINACH AND MUSHROOMS

SERVES 4

SERVING SIZE
1²/₃ cups
(400 mL)

IMMUNE-
BOOSTING
FOODS: ③

This is my absolute go-to dish when everyone is working from home or attending virtual school. I usually make a double portion of this bow tie pasta dish on Sunday so any one of my children can heat and eat it during the busy work week.

8 oz (250 g) 100% whole wheat farfalle

1 tbsp (15 mL) olive oil

2 cloves garlic, minced

8 oz (250 g) mushrooms, trimmed and thinly sliced

3 cups (750 mL) baby spinach

1 can (10 oz/300 g) chunk white chicken breast packed in water, drained and rinsed

1 cup (250 mL) part-skim ricotta cheese

½ cup (125 mL) tomato-based pasta sauce

1 Fill a large pot three-quarters with water and bring to a boil over high heat. Add the pasta and cook until al dente, 11 minutes. Drain and set aside.

2 In the same pot, heat the olive oil over medium heat. When the oil is shimmering, add the garlic and cook until fragrant, 30 seconds. Add the mushrooms and cook, stirring occasionally, until softened, about 5 minutes. Add the spinach and cook, stirring occasionally, until wilted, 3 minutes. Remove from the heat and let the vegetable mixture cool in the pot for at least 5 minutes.

3 Add the pasta and chicken to the vegetable mixture and toss to combine. Add the ricotta cheese and pasta sauce and toss to evenly coat.

4 Divide the pasta equally among four bowls. Serve immediately.

TOBY'S TIP | There is also no salt added to this recipe, as there is enough from the chicken breast, ricotta cheese and pasta sauce. If you need more seasoning, start with ⅛ tsp (0.5 mL) ground black pepper.

Herbed Turkey Chickpea Meatballs WITH YOGURT SAUCE

SERVES 6

SERVING SIZE
5 meatballs plus
1/4 cup (60 mL)
sauce

IMMUNE-
BOOSTING
FOODS: ③

The nutrients in chickpeas, like folate, fiber, magnesium and potassium, complement those in turkey, like B-vitamins, zinc and selenium, which amps up the immune-boosting power of each food. In all, this powerhouse recipe provides three immune-boosting foods.

2 baking sheets coated with nonstick cooking spray

Food processor or blender

SAUCE

1½ cups (375 mL) nonfat plain Greek yogurt

Zest and juice of 1 lemon

¼ cup (60 mL) chopped parsley

2 cloves garlic, minced

¼ tsp (1 mL) salt

⅛ tsp (0.5 mL) ground black pepper

MEATBALLS

1 can (14 to 19 oz/398 to 540 mL) low-sodium chickpeas, drained and rinsed

1 yellow onion, halved and thinly sliced

Juice of 1 lemon

¼ cup (60 mL) parsley

1 large egg, beaten

2 cloves garlic, crushed

½ tsp (2 mL) smoked paprika

½ tsp (2 mL) salt

⅛ tsp (0.5 mL) ground black pepper

1 lb (500 g) lean ground turkey

½ cup (125 mL) dry unseasoned bread crumbs

¼ cup (60 mL) olive oil

---

1 TO MAKE THE SAUCE: In a medium bowl, whisk together the yogurt, lemon zest and juice, parsley, garlic, salt and pepper until combined. Cover and place in the refrigerator to let the flavors combine for at least 20 minutes and up to 5 days.

2 TO MAKE THE MEATBALLS: Preheat the oven to 375°F (190°C).

3 In the bowl of the food processor or blender, add the chickpeas, onion, lemon juice, parsley, egg, garlic, smoked paprika, salt and pepper. Process or blend on High until well combined, about 1 minute.

4 Transfer the chickpea mixture to a large mixing bowl. Add the turkey and bread crumbs and stir to combine.

5 Using clean hands, scoop 1 heaping tbsp (15 mL) of the turkey-chickpea mixture and roll into a ball. Place on a clean plate and repeat, keeping meatballs about ½ inch (1 cm) apart. You should have a total of 30 meatballs. Cover and refrigerate for at least 30 minutes.

6 In a large skillet, heat 2 tbsp (30 mL) of the oil over medium heat. When the oil is shimmering, add half of the meatballs and cook, browning all sides, about 6 minutes. Transfer half of the meatballs to one of the prepared baking sheets, leaving 1 inch (2.5 cm) between meatballs.

7 Bake until the meatballs are golden brown and an instant-read thermometer inserted into two or three meatballs registers 165°F (74°C), 15 to 18 minutes. Remove the baking sheet from the oven and let the meatballs cool for 10 minutes. Repeat with the remaining oil, meatballs and prepared baking sheet.

8 To serve, divide the meatballs among six plates and serve with 1/4 cup (60 mL) of the yogurt sauce on the side.

> **TOBY'S TIP** | Replace the parsley with the same amount of cilantro or dill, or use a different fresh herb of your choice.

Chicken, Mushroom and Avocado Quesadilla

SERVES 4

SERVING SIZE
1 quesadilla

IMMUNE-
BOOSTING
FOODS: ②

Quesadillas are a go-to lunch or dinner. Fill them with leftovers — like chili or chicken — or whip up this version with mushrooms, chicken and avocado. Don't forget the cheese! It binds your quesadilla together to keep all the ingredients from falling out!

1 tbsp (15 mL) olive oil

8 oz (250 g) white button mushrooms, trimmed and thinly sliced

1/4 cup (60 mL) cilantro, chopped

4 large whole wheat tortillas

1 cup (250 mL) reduced-fat Monterey Jack cheese

1 cup (250 mL) rotisserie chicken, skin removed and chopped

1 avocado, pitted, peeled and thinly sliced

1 cup (250 mL) store-bought salsa

1 In a large skillet, heat the olive oil over medium heat. When the oil is shimmering, add the mushrooms and cook until softened, about 5 minutes. Add the cilantro and cook until slightly wilted, about 1 minute more. Spoon the mushroom mixture into a clean bowl.

2 Coat the same large skillet with nonstick cooking spray and heat over medium-low heat. When the oil is shimmering, place 1 tortilla in the center of the skillet. Add 2 tbsp (30 mL) of the cheese over half the tortilla, top the same half with 1/4 cup (60 mL) of the chicken, 1/4 cup (60 mL) of the mushroom mixture, several avocado slices, and finally an additional 2 tbsp (30 mL) of the cheese. Fold the empty half of the tortilla over the ingredients and cook until the cheese has slightly melted, 3 to 4 minutes on each side. Transfer the quesadilla to a dinner plate. Repeat with the remaining 3 tortillas.

3 Using a pizza slicer or sharp knife, slice the quesadillas into three even wedges. Spoon 1/4 cup (60 mL) of the salsa on the side of each quesadilla. Serve immediately.

> **TOBY'S TIP** | Before slicing avocado, rinse the outside with cool running water to remove any dirt.

Skillet Chicken
WITH ROSEMARY AND GRAPES

One easy trick to getting a chicken dinner on the table quickly is to cut the pieces of the chicken into smaller pieces. They cook faster, which means you'll have dinner ready even quicker!

SERVES 4

SERVING SIZE
1 cup (250 mL)

IMMUNE-
BOOSTING
FOODS: ①

1½ lbs (750 g) boneless skinless chicken breasts, cut into 1-inch (2.5 cm) strips

¼ tsp (1 mL) salt

¼ tsp (1 mL) ground black pepper

3 tbsp (45 mL) olive oil or canola oil

2 cups (500 mL) red or green seedless grapes

2 tsp (10 mL) dried rosemary

Zest of 1 lemon

2 tsp (10 mL) balsamic vinegar

1 Sprinkle both sides of the chicken with the salt and pepper.

2 In a large oven-safe skillet, heat 2 tbsp (30 mL) of the oil over medium heat. When the oil is shimmering, add the chicken and cook on all sides until an instant-read thermometer inserted in the chicken registers 165°F (74°C), 8 minutes. Transfer the chicken to a clean plate. Wipe the skillet with a paper towel.

3 In a medium bowl, add the grapes, rosemary, lemon zest and balsamic vinegar and toss to combine.

4 Preheat the oven to 375°F (190°C).

5 In the same large oven-safe skillet, heat the remaining 1 tbsp (15 mL) oil over medium heat. When the oil is shimmering, add the grape mixture and cook the grapes until warmed, gently tossing occasionally with a wooden spoon, 5 minutes. Transfer the pan to the oven and roast until the grapes have softened, 20 minutes. Using an oven mitt, carefully remove the pan from the oven and return to the stove over medium heat. Add the chicken to the grapes and gently toss to combine. Cook until the chicken is heated through, an additional 3 to 5 minutes.

6 Divide the chicken and grape mixture among four plates. Serve warm.

> **TOBY'S TIP** | Serve over a whole grain side like brown rice or Quinoa and Almond Pilaf (page 211).

TOBY'S TIP | You may find fig jam in the aisle with jellies, jams and preserves, but I have also found it in the fine cheeses section of the grocery. Fig jam tastes fantastic on whole wheat crackers with a small slice of cheese.

Chicken Breasts
WITH ORANGE-FIG SAUCE

This sauce takes 15 minutes to whip up while the chicken bakes. Worth every minute! Meet your new favorite weeknight dinner.

SERVING SIZE
1 chicken breast plus ⅓ cup (75 mL) sauce

IMMUNE-BOOSTING FOODS: ③

Large cast-iron skillet or large ovenproof skillet

CHICKEN

Four 5-oz (150 g) boneless skinless chicken breasts

¼ tsp (1 mL) salt

⅛ tsp (0.5 mL) ground black pepper

2 tbsp (30 mL) olive oil

SAUCE

2 tbsp (30 mL) olive oil

1 yellow onion, chopped

4 cloves garlic, minced

1 tbsp (15 mL) balsamic vinegar

1 tsp (5 mL) dried rosemary

1 cup (250 mL) low-sodium chicken broth

½ cup (125 mL) 100% orange juice

¼ cup (60 mL) fig jam

⅛ tsp (0.5 mL) salt

1 tbsp (15 mL) cornstarch

TO SERVE

¼ cup (60 mL) chopped fresh parsley

PREHEAT THE OVEN TO 400°F (200°C)

1 TO MAKE THE CHICKEN: Sprinkle both sides of the chicken breasts with the salt and pepper. In a large cast-iron skillet or ovenproof skillet, heat the oil over medium-high heat. When the oil is shimmering, add the chicken breasts and cook until slightly golden, about 4 minutes on each side. Transfer the skillet into the oven and cook until an instant-read thermometer inserted in the thickest part of each chicken breast registers 165°F (74°C), 15 minutes. Remove the skillet from the oven and set aside to rest for 10 minutes.

2 TO MAKE THE SAUCE: In a small saucepan, heat the oil over medium heat. When the oil is shimmering, add the onion and cook until translucent, about 3 minutes. Stir in the garlic, balsamic vinegar and rosemary and cook until fragrant, about 30 seconds. Whisk in ¾ cup (175 mL) of the chicken broth, then whisk in the orange juice, fig jam and salt. Increase the heat to high and bring the mixture to a boil. Reduce the heat to low and simmer, whisking occasionally, to allow the flavors to combine, about 10 minutes.

3 In a small bowl, whisk together the cornstarch and the remaining ¼ cup (60 mL) chicken broth. Add the cornstarch mixture to the saucepan and stir until the sauce thickens, 3 minutes.

4 TO SERVE: Divide the chicken among four plates and top with the sauce. Sprinkle with the parsley and serve warm.

Chicken Stir-Fry WITH
RED PEPPERS, BROCCOLI AND WALNUTS

Give your immune system a boost with this colorful stir-fry. Everyone in the family will enjoy this go-to dish!

1 cup (250 mL) long-grain brown rice

2¼ (560 mL) cups low-sodium chicken broth

2 tbsp (30 m) reduced-sodium soy sauce

1 tbsp (15 mL) unseasoned rice vinegar

2 tsp (10 mL) cornstarch

1 tsp (5 mL) honey

1 tsp (5 mL) fresh lime juice

¼ tsp (1 mL) ground ginger

1 lb (500 g) boneless skinless chicken breasts, cut into 1-inch (2.5 cm) cubes

¼ tsp (1 mL) salt

⅛ tsp (0.5 mL) ground black pepper

3 tbsp (45 mL) olive oil

2 red bell peppers, cut into ½-inch (1 cm) thick slices

4 cups (1 L) broccoli florets

¼ cup (60 mL) raw walnuts, coarsely chopped

SERVES 4

SERVING SIZE
About 2 cups
(500 mL) stir-fry
plus ½ cup
(125 mL) rice

IMMUNE-
BOOSTING
FOODS: ③

1 In a medium saucepan, bring the rice and 2 cups (500 mL) of the broth to a boil over high heat. Reduce the heat to low and simmer, covered, until the broth is absorbed, 35 to 40 minutes. Fluff the rice with a fork.

2 In a small bowl, whisk together the remaining ¼ cup (60 mL) broth, soy sauce, rice vinegar, cornstarch, honey, lime juice and ground ginger.

3 Sprinkle both sides of the chicken with the salt and black pepper. In a large skillet or wok, heat 2 tbsp (30 mL) of the oil over medium heat. When the oil is shimmering, add the chicken and cook on all sides until an instant-read thermometer registers 165°F (74°C), about 8 minutes. Transfer the chicken to a clean plate.

4 Heat the remaining 1 tbsp (15 mL) oil in the same skillet or wok. When the oil is shimmering, add the bell peppers and broccoli and cook until slightly softened, about 5 minutes. Add the broth mixture and increase the heat to high and bring to a boil, then reduce the heat to medium and cook until the sauce is slightly thickened, 1 minute. Add the chicken back into the skillet or wok and toss to evenly coat with the sauce. Sprinkle with the walnuts.

5 To serve, divide the rice among four plates and top with the chicken stir-fry. Serve warm.

Turkey and Asparagus Penne

All-in-one dishes that combine multiple food groups make leftovers a breeze. This dish brings together whole grains, lean protein and veggies for a complete, filling meal in a bowl.

SERVING SIZE
2⅓ cups
(575 mL)

IMMUNE-
BOOSTING
FOODS: ③

8 oz (250 g) dry whole wheat penne

Olive oil

1 lb (500 g) turkey breast cutlets, cut into bite-size pieces

1 yellow onion, chopped

4 cloves garlic, minced

8 oz (250 g) mushrooms, thinly sliced

2 tbsp (30 mL) all-purpose flour

¾ cup (175 mL) reduced-fat (2%) milk

¾ cup (175 mL) low-sodium chicken or vegetable broth

¼ cup (60 mL) grated Parmesan cheese

Zest and juice of 1 lemon

¼ tsp (1 mL) salt

⅛ tsp (0.5 mL) ground black pepper

1 lb (500 g) asparagus, trimmed and cut into 1-inch (2.5 cm) pieces

1 Fill a large pot three-quarters with water and bring to a boil over high heat. Stir in the pasta and return to a boil. Reduce the heat to medium-low and simmer, uncovered, until the pasta is al dente, about 8 minutes. Reserve ½ cup (125 mL) of the pasta water. Drain the pasta, then transfer to a large bowl and set aside.

2 In a large skillet, heat 2 tbsp (30 mL) olive oil over medium heat. When the oil is shimmering, add the turkey and cook, turning halfway through, until almost cooked through, about 6 minutes. Transfer the turkey to a clean plate.

3 In the same skillet, heat 1 tbsp (15 mL) olive oil over medium heat. Add the onion and cook until soft and translucent, about 3 minutes. Add the garlic and continue cooking until fragrant, 30 seconds. Add the mushrooms and cook until tender, about 6 minutes.

4 Sprinkle the vegetables with the flour and toss to combine. Stir in the milk, broth, cheese, lemon juice, salt and pepper. Add the cooked turkey and asparagus and bring to a boil over high heat, stirring occasionally. If the dish is a little dry, add 1 to 2 tbsp (15 to 30 mL) of the reserved pasta water. Reduce the heat to medium-low, cover and cook the vegetables and turkey through, about 15 minutes.

5 Stir the cooked pasta into the vegetable mixture and cook until heated through, 2 minutes. Sprinkle the pasta dish with the lemon zest and toss to combine.

6 Divide the pasta among four dinner plates. Serve warm.

Beef and Rice–Stuffed Peppers

This delicious, well-balanced family meal is perfect for meal prepping and stashing extras in your freezer for busy weeknights.

SERVES 4

SERVING SIZE
2 pepper halves

IMMUNE-
BOOSTING
FOODS: ④

Two 13- by 9-inch (33 by 23 cm) glass baking dishes coated with nonstick cooking spray

½ cup (125 mL) dried long-grain brown rice

1¼ cup (300 mL) low-sodium beef broth

1 tbsp (15 mL) olive oil

1 yellow onion, chopped

2 cloves garlic, minced

8 oz (250 g) lean ground beef, at least 90% lean

8 oz (250 g) cremini mushrooms

1 can (14 oz/498 mL) diced tomatoes, with juice

1 tsp (5 mL) dried parsley

½ tsp (2 mL) dried thyme

½ tsp (2 mL) dried basil

¼ tsp (1 mL) salt

⅛ tsp (0.5 mL) ground black pepper

4 red bell peppers, cut lengthwise, membranes and seeds removed

½ cup (125 mL) reduced-fat shredded Cheddar cheese

PREHEAT THE OVEN TO 350°F (180°C)

1 In a medium saucepan, bring the brown rice and broth to a boil over high heat. Reduce the heat to low, cover the pan and simmer until the rice is tender and the liquid is absorbed, 40 minutes. Fluff with a fork.

2 In a medium skillet, heat the oil over medium heat. Add the onion and garlic and cook until the onion is translucent and the garlic is fragrant, about 3 minutes. Add the ground beef and cook, breaking up the meat with a wooden spoon, until the meat is no longer pink, 5 minutes. Add the mushrooms and cook until the liquid is released, about 5 minutes. Add the tomatoes with juice, parsley, thyme, basil, salt and black pepper and stir to combine. Bring the mixture to a boil. Reduce the heat and simmer uncovered, stirring occasionally, about 10 minutes. Add the cooked rice and stir to combine. Set the mixture aside and let cool for 10 minutes.

3 Spoon the mixture into each pepper and, using clean hands, gently press down to lightly pack. Arrange the peppers 1 inch (2.5 cm) apart in the baking dish. Top each pepper with 1 tbsp (15 mL) of the shredded cheese. Cover loosely with aluminum foil.

4 Bake until the peppers are soft and the cheese has melted, 20 minutes. Remove the baking dish from the oven and let cool for 10 minutes before serving. Serve warm or store in the refrigerator in a sealable container for up to 4 days.

Beef and Mushroom Bolognese WITH PENNE

Mushrooms and garlic blend beautifully with the beef in this Bolognese. Not only do the flavors combine well, but you're getting three immune-boosting foods in one dish. It's a win-win all around!

2 tbsp (30 mL) olive oil

1 stalk celery, chopped

1 carrot, chopped

1 yellow onion, chopped

3 cloves garlic, minced

1 lb (500 g) lean ground beef (at least 90% lean)

6 oz (175 g) portobello mushroom caps, chopped

1 cup (250 mL) low-sodium beef broth

1 cup (250 mL) reduced-fat (2%) milk

1/8 tsp (0.5 mL) ground nutmeg

1 can (28 oz/796 mL) diced tomatoes, with juice

1/4 cup (60 mL) tomato paste

1 tbsp (15 mL) apple cider vinegar

1 tbsp (15 mL) dried parsley flakes

1 tsp (5 mL) dried basil

1 tsp (5 mL) dried oregano

1 tsp (5 mL) honey

3 bay leaves

1/4 tsp (1 mL) salt

1/4 tsp (1 mL) ground black pepper

12 oz (375 g) whole wheat penne or ziti

1/3 cup (75 mL) grated Parmesan cheese

SERVES 6

SERVING SIZE
1 1/2 cups
(375 mL) pasta
plus 1 cup
(250 mL) sauce

IMMUNE-BOOSTING FOODS: ③

1 Heat the olive oil in a large sauté pan over medium heat. When the oil is shimmering, add the celery, carrot and onion and cook until the vegetables have softened, about 5 minutes. Add the garlic and cook until fragrant, 1 minute more. Add the ground beef and mushrooms and cook until the meat is no longer pink, breaking up the pieces of beef with the back of a wooden spoon, about 8 minutes.

2 Add the beef broth and bring the mixture to a boil over high heat. Lower the heat to medium-low and cook, uncovered, until some of the liquid is evaporated, about 10 minutes. Add the milk and nutmeg and bring the mixture to a boil over high heat. Lower the heat to medium-low and cook, uncovered, stirring occasionally, until some more of the liquid is evaporated, about 10 minutes.

3 Add the tomatoes with juice, tomato paste, apple cider vinegar, parsley, basil, oregano, honey, bay leaves, salt and black pepper. Bring the mixture to a boil over high heat, and then lower the heat to low and simmer, covered, until the sauce and flavors combine, about 30 minutes. Uncover the sauté pan and continue cooking, stirring occasionally, until the sauce thickens, 30 minutes more.

4 While the sauce thickens, fill a large pot with 4 to 6 quarts (4 to 6 L) of water and bring to a boil over high heat. Add the penne and stir to combine. Return to a boil, then lower the heat to medium-low and simmer until the pasta is al dente, 10 minutes, stirring occasionally. Drain the pasta and place in a bowl. Cover to keep warm.

5 Once the sauce has thickened, add the Parmesan cheese to the sauce and stir to combine. Discard the bay leaves before serving.

6 To serve, place the pasta in a serving bowl and top with the sauce. Serve warm.

TOBY'S TIP To cut back on the sodium, check the labels and choose low-sodium or no-added-sodium diced tomatoes and tomato paste.

TOBY'S TIPS | Save on prep time by using leftover steak or beef cut into bite-size pieces.

Store leftover pizza wrapped in aluminum foil in the refrigerator for up to 4 days. Reheat in the oven at 350°F (180°C) for 10 minutes.

Steak Pizza
WITH PEPPERS AND ONIONS

SERVES 8

SERVING SIZE
$\frac{1}{4}$ pizza

IMMUNE-
BOOSTING
FOODS: ②

Steak is a favorite dinner in my home, and I have fun finding different ways for us to enjoy it. Lean steak, like tenderloin, provides the benefits of this red meat without much saturated fat.

Large grill pan or skillet coated with nonstick cooking spray

2 baking sheets coated with nonstick cooking spray

$\frac{1}{4}$ cup (60 mL) olive oil

1 clove garlic, minced

1 tsp (5 mL) smoked paprika

$\frac{1}{4}$ tsp (1 mL) ground cumin

$\frac{1}{4}$ tsp (1 mL) salt

$\frac{1}{8}$ tsp (0.5 mL) ground black pepper

12 oz (375 g) steak tenderloin, sliced into $\frac{1}{2}$-inch (1 cm) strips

1 red bell pepper, sliced into $\frac{1}{4}$-inch (0.5 cm) strips

1 yellow onion, thinly sliced

Two 11-inch (28 cm) prepared thin-crust pizza crusts, preferably 100% whole wheat

$1\frac{1}{2}$ cups (375 mL) store-bought marinara sauce

$1\frac{1}{2}$ cups (375 mL) shredded part-skim mozzarella cheese

1 In a medium bowl, whisk together the oil, garlic, smoked paprika, cumin, $\frac{1}{8}$ tsp (0.5 mL) of the salt and the pepper. Add the steak and turn to evenly coat. Cover the bowl and refrigerate for at least 30 minutes and up to overnight.

2 Remove the steak from the refrigerator. Heat the prepared grill pan or skillet over medium-high heat. When the oil is shimmering, add the steak and cook, turning once, until an instant-read thermometer inserted in the steak registers 145°F (63°C), 10 minutes. Transfer the steak to a cutting board and let cool for 10 minutes. Cut into bite-size pieces.

3 Preheat the oven to 400°F (200°C). Without wiping clean, spray the grill pan or skillet with cooking spray and place over medium heat.

4 Add the bell pepper and onion and cook until the vegetables soften, about 5 minutes. Add the steak pieces and the remaining $\frac{1}{8}$ tsp (0.5 mL) salt to the vegetables and toss to combine.

5 Place one pizza crust onto each of the prepared baking sheets. Divide the marinara sauce among the crusts and spread evenly with the back of a spoon. Sprinkle the cheese and the steak mixture over each crust.

6 Bake on separate racks until the cheese has melted, 10 minutes. Remove the pizzas from the oven and let cool for 10 minutes. Cut each pizza into eight slices and serve.

Beef and Sweet Potato Bowls

Bowls have become very popular and are fun to make, like this take on Korean bibimbap! Make sure your bowls include a whole grain or starch, lots of veggies and a lean protein for a nicely balanced meal.

SERVING SIZE
1 bowl

IMMUNE-BOOSTING FOODS: ⑤

Baking sheet coated with nonstick cooking spray

Grill pan or sauté pan

½ cup (125 mL) low-sodium soy sauce

⅓ cup (75 mL) unseasoned rice vinegar

1 tbsp (15 mL) honey

1 tbsp (15 mL) sesame oil

2 tsp (10 mL) sriracha

½ tsp (2 mL) ground ginger

2 cloves garlic, minced

1 lb (500 g) top sirloin steak

Olive oil

1 tsp (5 mL) fish sauce

2 sweet potatoes (about 1½ lbs/750 g), peeled and cut into ½-inch (1 cm) cubes

5 oz (150 g) baby spinach

¾ cup (175 mL) dry quinoa

1⅓ cup (325 mL) low-sodium vegetable broth

2 limes, quartered

1 In a large bowl, whisk together the soy sauce, rice vinegar, honey, sesame oil, sriracha, ginger and garlic. Add the steak and turn to coat evenly. Cover and place in the refrigerator to marinate for at least 30 minutes and up to 24 hours.

2 Preheat the oven to 425°F (220°C).

3 In a medium bowl, whisk together 1 tbsp (15 mL) olive oil and the fish sauce. Add the sweet potatoes and toss to coat. Place the sweet potatoes in a single layer on the prepared baking sheet. Cook until slightly browned, about 15 minutes, flipping once halfway through. Remove the baking sheet from the oven and let cool for at least 10 minutes. Decrease the temperature of the oven to 400°F (200°C).

4 Place the prepared grill pan or sauté pan over medium-high heat. When the oil is shimmering, shake off excess marinade from the steak and discard the marinade. Add the steak to the grill pan or sauté pan and cook until slightly browned, 4 to 5 minutes on each side. Transfer the pan to the oven and cook the steak until it reaches an internal temperature of 145°F (63°C). Set the steak on a cutting board to rest for 10 minutes and then cut against the grain into 1-inch (2.5 cm) slices.

5 In a medium saucepan, heat 1 tbsp (15 mL) olive oil over medium heat until shimmering. Add the spinach and cook, stirring occasionally, until wilted, 3 minutes. Transfer the spinach from the saucepan onto a clean plate.

6 In the same medium saucepan, add the quinoa and toast over medium heat, stirring regularly, for about 2 minutes. Add the vegetable broth and bring the mixture to a boil over high heat. Lower the heat to low and simmer, covered, until the liquid is absorbed, 15 minutes. Remove the saucepan from the heat and fluff with a fork.

7 To assemble the bowls, spoon $\frac{1}{2}$ cup (125 mL) of the quinoa onto the bottom of each bowl. Top with one-fourth of the spinach, about $\frac{3}{4}$ cup (175 mL) of the sweet potato and about 4 oz (125 g) of the steak. Serve with lime wedges to be squeezed on before eating.

TOBY'S TIP | You can swap the fish sauce with low-sodium soy sauce.

Golden Pork Chops

IMMUNE-
BOOSTING
FOODS: ②

Boneless pork chops are a lean cut of meat that can be part of a healthy eating plan. Marinating the pork in flavorful ingredients like turmeric, honey and orange adds fabulous flavor and several immune-boosting foods.

Juice and zest of 1 orange

Olive oil

1 tbsp (15 mL) honey

2 tsp (10 mL) ground turmeric

¼ tsp (1 mL) salt

⅛ tsp (0.5 mL) ground black pepper

Four 4 oz (125 g) boneless pork chops

1 shallot, chopped

1 In a medium bowl, whisk together the orange juice and zest, 3 tbsp (45 mL) olive oil, the honey, turmeric, salt and black pepper. Place the pork chops in the bowl and turn to coat evenly. Cover the bowl and place in the refrigerator for at least 30 minutes and up to 24 hours to marinate.

2 Heat 1 tbsp (15 mL) olive oil in a large sauté pan over medium heat. When the oil is shimmering, add the shallots and cook until translucent, 3 minutes. Remove the pork chops from the marinade, shaking off any excess, and discard the marinade. Add the pork chops to the pan and cook until the internal temperature reaches 145°F (63°C), 4 to 5 minutes on each side.

3 Transfer the pork chops from the pan to a plate and let rest for 10 minutes before serving.

> **TOBY'S TIPS**
>
> Serve the pork chops with Sautéed Spinach with Fennel and Red Onions (page 223) and Jasmine Rice with Peas and Lentils (page 216).
>
> To save time with prep, marinate the pork the night before.

Yogurt Marinated Pork Kebabs

An immune-boosting food, Greek yogurt not only tastes great, but its acidity helps marinate meat, like the pork in this recipe. Garlic and mint combine with the yogurt for an easy and delicious Mediterranean-inspired marinade that's sure to please.

IMMUNE-
BOOSTING
FOODS: ③

8 wood or metal skewers

Grill pan or grill

½ cup (125 mL) fresh mint leaves, chopped

½ cup (125 mL) reduced-fat (2%) plain Greek yogurt

2 tbsp (30 mL) dry white wine

3 cloves garlic, minced

¼ tsp (1 mL) salt

⅛ tsp (0.5 mL) ground black pepper

1 lb (500 g) pork tenderloin, cut into 1-inch (2.5 cm) cubes for a total of 16 pieces

2 yellow onions

1 medium red bell pepper, cut into 2-inch (5 cm) pieces

16 grape tomatoes

1 In a medium bowl, whisk together the mint, yogurt, wine, garlic, salt and black pepper. Add the pork cubes and toss to evenly coat. Cover the bowl and refrigerate for exactly 1 hour.

2 If you are using wooden skewers, soak them in water for at least 10 minutes.

3 Halve each onion lengthwise and halve again crosswise. Cut each of the chunks in half for a total of 16 onion chunks.

4 Preheat a grill pan or a grill over medium heat.

5 Remove the pork from the marinade, allowing the excess to drip off. Discard the marinade.

6 Thread each skewer with 1 piece each of pork, onion, bell pepper and tomato, then repeat the pattern one more time.

7 Transfer the skewers to the preheated grill pan or grill, turning them several times, until the pork is browned and an instant-read thermometer inserted in the pork registers 145°F (63°C), 12 to 15 minutes.

8 To serve, place two skewers on each of four plates. Serve warm.

TOBY'S TIPS Swap the pork for lean beef, lamb, chicken or tofu.

Serve with Bell Pepper and Mozzarella Couscous (page 213).

Brown Rice
WITH SPINACH AND MUSHROOMS

SERVES 6

SERVING SIZE
3/4 cup (175 mL)

IMMUNE-
BOOSTING
FOODS: ③

Vegetables provide a variety of antioxidants and phytonutrients, which are natural plant compounds that help prevent disease and keep you healthy, so it's important to find ways to add more veggies to your diet. This brown rice dish gets a veggie boost both for flavor and to help your immune system stay healthy.

2 tbsp (30 mL) olive oil

1 yellow onion, chopped

2 cloves garlic, minced

8 oz (250 g) cremini mushrooms, chopped

1 cup (250 mL) dry long-grain brown rice

2¼ cups (560 mL) low-sodium vegetable broth

½ tsp (2 mL) dried oregano

½ tsp (2 mL) dried thyme

¼ tsp (1 mL) salt

⅛ tsp (0.5 mL) ground black pepper

3 cups (750 mL) baby spinach

1 In a medium saucepan, heat the oil over medium heat. When the oil is shimmering, add the onion and garlic and cook until soft and fragrant, 3 minutes. Add the mushrooms and cook until softened, about 5 minutes.

2 Add the rice, broth, oregano, thyme, salt and pepper to the vegetable mixture and bring to a boil over high heat. Reduce the heat to medium-low and simmer, covered, until the rice is tender, 40 minutes. Add the spinach and cook until wilted, 2 minutes. Stir to incorporate.

3 To serve, divide among six bowls. Serve warm.

> **TOBY'S TIP** | Swap the brown rice for quinoa but simmer for only 15 minutes.

Quinoa and Almond Pilaf

Although technically a seed, nutritionally quinoa is considered a whole grain. In this recipe, crunchy almonds, sweet raisins and a tangy vinaigrette come together for an outstanding side.

SERVING SIZE
2/3 cup (150 mL)

IMMUNE-
BOOSTING
FOODS: ②

DRESSING

Juice of 1 lemon

1 tbsp (15 mL) white wine vinegar

1/2 tsp (2 mL) dried thyme

1/2 tsp (2 mL) dried oregano

1/4 tsp (1 mL) salt

1/8 tsp (0.5 mL) ground black pepper

1/4 cup (60 mL) olive oil

SALAD

1 tbsp (15 mL) olive oil

2 shallots, chopped

2 cloves garlic, minced

1 cup (250 mL) low-sodium vegetable broth

1 cup (250 mL) water

1 cup (250 mL) dry quinoa

1/4 cup (60 mL) raw almonds, coarsely chopped

1/2 cup (125 mL) fresh parsley, chopped

1/2 cup (125 mL) raisins

1 TO MAKE THE DRESSING: In a small bowl, whisk together the lemon juice, vinegar, thyme, oregano, salt and pepper. Whisking continuously, slowly drizzle in the oil until incorporated.

2 TO MAKE THE SALAD: In a medium saucepan, heat the oil over medium heat. When the oil is shimmering, add the shallots and cook until translucent, about 3 minutes. Add garlic and continue cooking until fragrant, 30 seconds. Add the broth, water and quinoa and bring to a boil over high heat. Reduce the heat to medium-low and simmer, covered, until the liquid has been absorbed, 12 to 15 minutes. Remove the saucepan from the heat and let cool for 10 minutes. Fluff the quinoa with a fork.

3 In a small saucepan, heat the almonds over medium-low heat until toasted, about 5 minutes. Transfer the toasted almonds to a small bowl and set aside to cool slightly.

4 In a medium serving bowl, add the quinoa, almonds, parsley and raisins and toss to combine. Drizzle in the dressing and toss to coat evenly. Serve warm.

TOBY'S TIP | This side dish can be served cold or warm.

Roasted Bell Pepper and Mozzarella Couscous

SERVES 6

SERVING SIZE
$^1/_2$ cup (125 mL)

IMMUNE-
BOOSTING
FOODS: ①

I love dressing up side dishes with delicious and immune-boosting ingredients. Using store-bought roasted red bell peppers adds a really nice flavor without the trouble of roasting your own.

1¼ cups (300 mL) water

1 cup (250 mL) couscous, preferably whole wheat

3 oz (90 g) store-bought roasted red bell peppers, diced

4 oz (125 g) mozzarella, cut into 1-inch (2.5 cm) cubes

2 tbsp (30 mL) chopped fresh basil

2 tbsp (30 mL) chopped fresh parsley

2 tbsp (30 mL) extra virgin olive oil

¼ tsp (1 mL) salt

⅛ (0.5 mL) tsp ground black pepper

1 In a medium saucepan, bring the water to a boil. Stir in the couscous, cover the pan, and remove from the heat for 5 minutes. Fluff the couscous with a fork.

2 In a medium bowl, add the couscous, roasted red bell peppers, mozzarella, basil, parsley, oil, salt and black pepper. Cover the bowl and refrigerate for at least 15 minutes and up to 24 hours. Serve chilled.

TOBY'S TIP | Swap the couscous for quinoa and use 2 cups (500 mL) of water. Bring the mixture to a boil over high heat and then lower the heat to medium-low and simmer until the quinoa is cooked through, 15 minutes.

Creamy Farro
WITH GARLIC AND SPINACH

Farro is an ancient strain of wheat that's been around for centuries. It has a pleasant chewy texture and slightly nutty flavor. You can find pearled farro that cooks up quicker, but the whole grain farro called for in this recipe takes a bit longer to cook and has more fiber.

2 tbsp (30 mL) olive oil

5 oz (150 g) baby spinach

3 garlic cloves, minced

1¾ cups (425 mL) farro

4 cups (1 L) low-sodium vegetable broth or chicken broth

1 cup (250 mL) water

¼ tsp (1 mL) salt

⅛ tsp (0.5 mL) ground black pepper

½ cup (125 mL) shredded part-skim mozzarella cheese

¼ cup (60 mL) Parmesan cheese

SERVES 6

SERVING SIZE
¾ cups (175 mL)

IMMUNE-BOOSTING FOODS: ②

1 In a medium saucepan, heat 1 tbsp (15 mL) of the oil over medium heat. When the oil is shimmering, add the spinach and garlic and sauté until the spinach is wilted and the garlic is fragrant, about 3 minutes.

2 Add the remaining 1 tbsp (15 mL) oil to the saucepan and heat for about 1 minute. Add the farro and toast until light brown, about 2 minutes. Add the broth, water, salt and black pepper and bring to a boil over high heat. Reduce the heat to medium-low and simmer gently, covered, until the liquid is absorbed and the farro is tender, 30 minutes.

3 Drain off any excess liquid. Stir in the mozzarella and Parmesan cheeses and serve warm.

> **TOBY'S TIP** | Farro can be stored in a cool, dry, dark place for up to 6 months or in the freezer for up to 1 year.

Jasmine Rice
WITH PEAS AND LENTILS

SERVES 6

SERVING SIZE
1 cup (250 mL)

IMMUNE-
BOOSTING
FOODS: ③

It's a good idea to switch up the variety of grains you're eating. That's when jasmine rice comes in handy. This long-grain Asian rice grows mainly in Thailand, Cambodia, Laos and Vietnam and is a staple in many countries. It has a unique aroma, flavor and texture that can be incorporated with a variety of other ingredients.

1 cup (250 mL) dry white jasmine rice

2 cups (500 mL) low-sodium vegetable broth

2 tbsp (30 mL) olive oil

1 yellow onion, chopped

3 cloves garlic, minced

1 cup (250 mL) canned low-sodium brown lentils, drained and rinsed

1 cup (250 mL) canned low-sodium peas, drained and rinsed

1 tsp (5 mL) dried oregano

1 tsp (5 mL) ground cumin

¼ tsp (1 mL) ground turmeric

¼ tsp (1 mL) ground coriander

¼ tsp (1 mL) ancho chile powder

¼ tsp (1 mL) salt

1 In a medium saucepan, add the rice and vegetable broth and bring to a boil over high heat. Reduce the heat to medium-low and simmer, covered, until the rice is tender and cooked through, 20 minutes. Fluff the rice with a fork.

2 In a large sauté pan, heat the oil over medium heat. When the oil is shimmering, add the onion and garlic and cook until the onion is translucent and the garlic is fragrant, 3 minutes. Add the lentils, peas, oregano, cumin, turmeric, coriander, ancho chile powder and salt and toss to combine. Reduce the heat to medium-low and cook until heated through, 3 minutes. Add the cooked rice to the pan and toss to incorporate.

3 Transfer the rice to a serving bowl and serve warm.

> **TOBY'S TIP** | You can swap in frozen peas, but make sure to cook the peas according to the package directions before adding to the dish.

Bulgur
WITH GINGER AND ORANGE

SERVING SIZE
About 1 cup
(250 mL)

IMMUNE-
BOOSTING
FOODS: ④

This ancient grain is a form of whole wheat that has been around for thousands of years. Bulgur has a nutty flavor and chewy texture and cooks up just like rice – just combine it with water or broth and cook for the designated amount of time.

Olive oil

1 yellow onion, chopped

3 cloves garlic, minced

1 tsp (5 mL) grated fresh ginger

1 cup (250 mL) 100% orange juice or juice of freshly squeezed oranges

2 cups (500 mL) low-sodium vegetable broth

1½ cups (375 mL) dry bulgur

6 tbsp (90 mL) slivered almonds

1 tbsp (15 mL) unseasoned rice vinegar

1 tbsp (15 mL) reduced-sodium soy sauce

2 tsp (10 mL) honey

½ tsp (2 mL) Dijon mustard

1 In a medium saucepan, heat 2 tbsp (30 mL) olive oil over medium heat. When the oil is shimmering, add the onion and cook until soft and translucent, about 3 minutes. Add in the garlic and ginger, and continue cooking until fragrant, an additional 30 seconds. Add the orange juice, vegetable broth and bulgur and bring to a boil over high heat. Reduce the heat to medium-low and simmer, covered, until the liquid has been absorbed and the bulgur is tender, 25 to 30 minutes. Remove from the heat. Fluff the bulgur with a fork and let cool for 10 minutes.

2 While the bulgur is simmering, in a small saucepan, add the almonds and cook over medium-low heat until toasted, about 5 minutes. Transfer the almonds to a small bowl and let cool for 5 minutes.

3 In a small bowl, whisk together the vinegar, soy sauce, honey and mustard. While whisking vigorously, slowly drizzle in the remaining 2 tbsp (30 mL) olive oil. Drizzle the dressing over the bulgur and toss to evenly coat.

4 Transfer the bulgur to a serving bowl and sprinkle with toasted almonds. Serve warm.

> **TOBY'S TIP** | To make this dish vegan, swap the honey for the same amount of agave syrup.

Steamed Asparagus
WITH LEMON BUTTER

SERVING SIZE
About 3 oz (90 g)

IMMUNE-
BOOSTING
FOODS: ①

When cooking vegetables, I like to let the vegetable be the star of the show. This asparagus dish has a light sauce, so you'll get a little extra flavor but also be able to taste the deliciousness of the vegetable.

1 lb (500 g) asparagus, washed and trimmed

2 tbsp (30 mL) unsalted butter

Zest of 1 lemon and juice of ½ lemon

¼ tsp (1 mL) salt

⅛ tsp (0.5 mL) ground black pepper

1 Fill a medium saucepan with 1 inch (2.5 cm) water and fit it with a steamer basket. Place the asparagus in the basket and bring the water to a boil over high heat. Reduce the heat to low, cover the pan, and steam until the asparagus is just tender, 12 minutes. Using tongs, remove the asparagus from the steamer basket and place on a clean plate.

2 In a large skillet, heat the butter, lemon zest, lemon juice, salt and pepper over medium heat, stirring to combine. When the butter is melted and hot, add the asparagus and toss to evenly coat with the sauce. Transfer the asparagus and butter sauce to a serving dish and serve warm.

> **TOBY'S TIP** When cooking healthy dishes, you don't have to give up butter! Use a small amount of the real deal to get the delicious mouthfeel and flavor you want without going overboard on calories and saturated fat.

Garlic Soy Mushrooms

SERVES 8

SERVING SIZE
½ cup (125 mL)

IMMUNE-
BOOSTING
FOODS: ②

Mix up your weeknight side by making it a mushroom night. This dish takes under 30 minutes to whip up, and you can use leftovers to make mushroom and cheese quesadillas or just heat and eat for lunch the next day.

2 tbsp (30 mL) olive oil or canola oil

3 cloves garlic, minced

2 lbs (1 kg) cremini mushrooms, thinly sliced

1 tbsp (15 mL) reduced-sodium soy sauce

1 tbsp (15 mL) balsamic vinegar

2 tsp (10 mL) toasted sesame oil

¼ cup (60 mL) fresh parsley, chopped

1 In a large skillet or sauté pan, heat the oil over medium heat. When the oil is shimmering, add the garlic and cook until fragrant, about 30 seconds.

2 Add the mushrooms, soy sauce and balsamic vinegar and cook, stirring occasionally, until the mushrooms are tender and some of the liquid has evaporated, about 15 minutes.

3 Remove from the heat and drizzle with the toasted sesame oil and sprinkle the parsley over the top. Serve warm.

> **TOBY'S TIP** | Make this dish gluten-free by substituting tamari or coconut aminos in place of the soy sauce.

Sautéed Spinach
WITH FENNEL AND RED ONION

SERVES 4

SERVING SIZE
1 cup (250 mL)

IMMUNE-
BOOSTING
FOODS: ②

Fennel is an easy-to-use vegetable that can be enjoyed raw or cooked. When raw it has a licorice-like flavor that becomes milder when cooked and is complemented beautifully when paired with cooked spinach and a splash of orange juice.

2 tbsp (30 mL) olive or canola oil

1 red onion, quartered and thinly sliced

2 cloves garlic, minced

1 tbsp (15 mL) unsalted butter

1 fennel bulb, trimmed, cored and sliced into ¼-inch (0.5 cm) pieces

8 oz (250 g) baby spinach

¼ cup (60 mL) basil leaves, cut into ribbons

2 tbsp (30 mL) 100% orange juice

¼ tsp (1 mL) salt

⅛ tsp (0.5 mL) ground black pepper

1 In large sauté pan, heat the olive oil over medium heat. When the oil is shimmering, add the onion and garlic and cook until the onion is translucent and the garlic is fragrant, about 3 minutes.

2 Add the butter and allow to melt for 1 minute, then add the fennel and cook until it has softened, about 5 minutes. Add the spinach and basil and cook until wilted, 3 to 4 minutes.

3 Add the orange juice, salt and black pepper and toss to combine. Serve warm.

TOBY'S TIPS

Swap the spinach for kale or use a combination of both.

To minimize food waste, keep the fronds (or top part) of the fennel to toss into a vegetable salad or to add to broth or soup.

Sweet Potato Mash

This family favorite will fill your home with the scent of cinnamon, maple syrup and toasted pecans. Once your family or neighbors smell the delicious aroma, they'll be begging for a taste.

SERVING SIZE
About ¾ cup
(175 mL)

IMMUNE-
BOOSTING
FOODS: ①

Baking sheet lined with aluminum foil	¼ cup (60 mL) reduced-fat (2%) milk
Immersion blender or blender	2 tbsp (30 mL) unsalted butter
4 lbs (2 kg) sweet potatoes (about 4 large potatoes)	1 tbsp (15 mL) 100% pure maple syrup
⅓ cup (75 mL) raw pecans, chopped	½ tsp (2 mL) cinnamon
	¼ tsp (1 mL) salt

PREHEAT THE OVEN TO 425°F (220°C)

1 Using a fork, poke a few holes in each of the sweet potatoes. Place the sweet potatoes on the prepared baking sheet and bake until the potatoes are tender, about 1 hour. Remove the sweet potatoes from the oven and let them cool for about 15 minutes.

2 Place the pecans in a small sauté pan over medium-low heat. Cook until the pecans are slightly toasted, being careful not to burn them, 5 minutes. Remove the pecans from the pan and set aside to cool slightly.

3 When the sweet potatoes are cool enough to handle, slice lengthwise and, using a spoon, scoop out the flesh and place in a large bowl. Add the milk, butter, maple syrup, cinnamon and salt. Blend using an immersion blender or add to a blender and blend on high speed.

4 Spoon the mashed potato mixture into a serving bowl and sprinkle with toasted pecans.

> **TOBY'S TIP** | To make the recipe vegan, swap the milk to soymilk and use a plant-based butter or non-dairy margarine.

Skillet Green Tea Vegetables

Green tea isn't just for sipping. In this dish, the green tea sauce flavors vegetables for a quick and easy side that goes with chicken, beef, pork, tofu and fish.

1/2 cup (125 mL) boiling water

1 green tea bag

Zest of 1 lemon

2 tsp (10 mL) cornstarch

1/4 tsp (1 mL) ground ginger

1 tsp (5 mL) sriracha

1/4 tsp (1 mL) salt

2 tbsp (30 mL) olive oil or canola oil

2 red bell peppers, cut into 1/2-inch (1 cm) wide slices

8 oz (250 g) cremini mushrooms, thinly sliced

2 cups (500 mL) cauliflower florets

2 cups (500 mL) broccoli florets

1 In a small bowl, pour the boiling water over the tea bag and steep for exactly 3 minutes. Remove the tea bag and discard. Add the lemon zest, cornstarch, ginger, sriracha and salt and whisk to combine.

2 In a large skillet, heat the oil over medium heat. When the oil is shimmering, add the bell peppers, mushrooms, cauliflower and broccoli and cook until slightly softened, 10 minutes. Add the green tea mixture and increase the heat to high. Bring to a boil then reduce the heat to medium and simmer until the sauce has thickened slightly, 1 minute.

3 To serve, divide the vegetables among four plates. Serve warm.

> **TOBY'S TIP** | Mix up the vegetables to use whichever you have leftover in your refrigerator or whatever your tastebuds desire. Vegetables provide a ton of nutrients to help keep your immune system in tip-top shape.

Roasted Brussels Sprouts
WITH GRAPES

SERVING SIZE
3/4 cup (175 mL)

IMMUNE-
BOOSTING
FOODS: ①

This delicious side dish combines the crunchy cabbage-like flavor of Brussels sprouts with the sweetness of oven-roasted grapes. It's a wonderful side to dress up plain grilled chicken or beef.

Rimmed baking sheet coated with nonstick cooking spray

2 cups (500 mL) seedless red grapes

2 tsp (10 mL) dried tarragon

Olive oil

1½ lbs (750 g) Brussels sprouts, trimmed and halved

2 tbsp (30 mL) balsamic vinegar

Zest of 1 lemon

¼ tsp (1 mL) salt

⅛ tsp (0.5 mL) ground black pepper

PREHEAT THE OVEN TO 425°F (220°C)

1 In a medium bowl, add the grapes and tarragon and toss to combine.

2 In a medium skillet, heat 1 tbsp (15 mL) olive oil over medium heat. When the oil is shimmering, add the grape mixture and cook, gently stirring occasionally, until the grapes are warmed, about 5 minutes. Remove the skillet from the heat and let cool for 5 minutes.

3 Place the Brussels sprouts in a large bowl. Add 2 tbsp (30 mL) olive oil, the balsamic vinegar, lemon zest, salt and pepper and toss to evenly coat. Add the grapes and gently toss to combine.

4 Spread the Brussels sprouts and grapes in a single layer on the prepared baking sheet. Roast until the Brussels sprouts are slightly browned, about 20 minutes, using a spatula to turn halfway through. Remove from the oven and transfer to a large serving bowl and serve.

> **TOBY'S TIP** | When buying Brussels sprouts, look for those that are firm and heavy for their size. The leaves should be tightly packed. Avoid those with discolored leaves, yellow leaves or black spots. Store in a plastic bag in the refrigerator for up to 7 days.

CHAPTER 10

DESSERTS

Chocolate-Dipped Walnuts

SERVING SIZE
¼ cup (60 mL)

IMMUNE-
BOOSTING
FOODS: ①

Looking for a *very* simple dessert? I've got you covered! This dessert takes 15 minutes to put together, and the refrigerator does the rest. It's a yummy way to sweeten up immune-boosting nuts — plus, everything just tastes better with chocolate!

Baking sheet lined with parchment paper or a silicone baking mat

½ cup (125 mL) 60% bittersweet (dark) chocolate chips

1 cup (250 mL) raw or unsalted dry roasted walnut halves

⅛ tsp (0.5 mL) kosher salt

1 In a small microwave-safe bowl, add the chocolate chips and microwave on High for 30 seconds. Stir, then microwave on High for another 30 seconds, or until melted.

2 Using a spoon, scoop some chocolate and hover the spoon above the bowl. Dip the walnut three-quarters of the way into the chocolate. Shake the walnut gently to remove any excess chocolate. Place the walnut onto the prepared baking sheet. Repeat with the remaining walnuts, placing them about 1 inch (2.5 cm) apart on the baking sheet. Sprinkle the salt evenly over the walnuts.

3 Transfer the baking sheet to the refrigerator and let the chocolate set for at least 30 minutes and up to 24 hours. Serve cold.

TOBY'S TIPS

Swap the walnuts for raw or unsalted dry roasted almonds or use a combination of both.

When buying dark chocolate, look for at least 60% cacao. The higher the percentage, the darker the chocolate.

Greek Yogurt Chocolate Mousse WITH STRAWBERRIES

SERVES 4

SERVING SIZE
About ⅔ cup
(150 mL)
chocolate mousse

IMMUNE-BOOSTING FOODS: ②

Greek yogurt is very adaptable because it takes on the flavor of whatever you stir into it. In this dessert, it's combined with luscious chocolate to make a creamy, decadent treat that can also be enjoyed as a healthy snack.

¼ cup (60 mL) low-fat (1%) milk

4 oz (125 g) semi-sweet chocolate, coarsely chopped

1 tbsp (15 mL) pure maple syrup

½ tsp (2 mL) vanilla extract

⅛ tsp (0.5 mL) Kosher salt

2 cups (500 mL) reduced-fat plain Greek yogurt

8 strawberries, stems removed and thinly sliced

8 mint leaves, for garnish

1 Fill a small saucepan with 2 inches (5 cm) of water. Fit a heatproof bowl on top of the saucepan, making sure the bottom of the bowl doesn't touch the water, to create a double boiler.

2 Bring the water to a boil over high heat and then reduce the heat to medium-low.

3 Place the milk into the bowl and heat, whisking occasionally. When the milk is heated through, 3 to 4 minutes, add the chocolate and whisk occasionally, until melted. Add the maple syrup, vanilla extract and salt and whisk to combine. Remove the double boiler from the heat and let cool for 10 minutes.

4 In a medium bowl, add the yogurt and slowly drizzle in the cooled chocolate while whisking. Whisk vigorously for about 1 minute until the chocolate mixture is incorporated.

5 Divide the mousse evenly among four small bowls and top each with 2 sliced strawberries and 2 mint leaves. Cover and refrigerate for at least 30 minutes and up to 2 hours to set. Serve cold.

> **TOBY'S TIPS**
>
> To add an additional immune-boosting food, sprinkle each bowl of mousse with 1 tbsp (15 mL) chopped almonds or walnuts.
>
> Use whatever chocolate you enjoy most: semi-sweet, dark or milk.

Orange Poached Pears

My mom used to serve poached pears on special holidays. As I got older, I didn't understand why poached pears should be reserved only for the holidays. Why not enjoy them any night of the week? Since having kids, I have added this dessert into my everyday dessert repertoire.

SERVING SIZE
2 pear halves plus
$^1/_2$ cup (125 mL)
frozen yogurt

IMMUNE-
BOOSTING
FOODS: ④

2 cups (500 mL) 100% orange juice

2 cups (500 mL) water

$^1/_4$ cup (60 mL) pure maple syrup

6 whole cloves

1 tsp (5 mL) grated fresh ginger

$^1/_2$ tsp (2 mL) ground nutmeg

$^1/_2$ tsp (2 mL) vanilla extract

$^1/_8$ tsp (0.5 mL) ground cardamom

4 firm ripe pears, halved and cored

$^1/_2$ tsp (2 mL) grated orange zest

$^1/_4$ cup (60 mL) raw walnuts, chopped

2 cups (500 mL) vanilla frozen yogurt

1 In a medium saucepan, add the orange juice, water, maple syrup, cloves, ginger, nutmeg, vanilla extract and cardamom and bring to a boil over high heat. Add the pears and reduce the heat to medium-low. Simmer until the pears are fork-tender, about 30 minutes. Using a slotted spoon, transfer the cooked pears into a large serving dish and cover with aluminum foil to keep warm.

2 In the same saucepan, add the grated orange zest to the remaining poaching liquid and bring to a boil over high heat. Reduce the heat to medium-low and cook until the liquid reduces by half, about 15 minutes. Remove the whole cloves and discard.

3 Drizzle the sauce over the poached pears and sprinkle the pears with the walnuts.

4 In each of four dessert bowls, add 2 pear halves with the sauce and top with $^1/_2$ cup (125 mL) frozen yogurt. Serve immediately.

> **TOBY'S TIP** | Swap the frozen yogurt for nonfat vanilla-flavored Greek yogurt.

Gingerbread Chia Pudding

These little chia seeds are packed with nutrition, notably fiber, protein, calcium and iron. They even help your immune system, as they contain inflammation-fighting omega-3 fats, which makes this pudding more than just dessert.

IMMUNE-
BOOSTING
FOODS: ②

Four 4 oz (125 mL) lidded jars

2 tbsp (30 mL) pure maple syrup

2 tsp (10 mL) unsulfured molasses

1 tsp (5 mL) vanilla extract

1 tsp (5 mL) ground cinnamon

¼ tsp (1 mL) grated fresh ginger

¼ tsp (1 mL) ground nutmeg

¼ tsp (1 mL) allspice

⅛ tsp (0.5 mL) salt

2 cups (500 mL) unsweetened almond milk or nonfat milk

½ cup (125 mL) chia seeds

¼ cup (60 mL) raw or unsalted roasted chopped pecans

¼ cup (60 mL) dark chocolate chips

1 In a medium bowl, whisk together the maple syrup, molasses, vanilla, cinnamon, ginger, nutmeg, allspice and salt. Slowly whisk in the almond milk until incorporated.

2 Pour about ½ cup (125 mL) of the almond milk mixture into each of the glass jars. Add 2 tbsp (30 mL) of the chia seeds into each jar and stir until well combined. Cover the jars and refrigerate for at least 8 hours and up to 24 hours.

3 To serve, open the jars and top each with 1 tbsp (15 mL) of the pecans and 1 tbsp (15 mL) of the dark chocolate chips. Serve immediately.

> **TOBY'S TIP** | Want even more flavor? Add sliced bananas and a drizzle of maple syrup before serving!

Chocolate Oat Cookies

These better-for-you ooey, gooey cookies use unsaturated canola oil instead of butter. They also contain immune-boosting rolled oats. Enjoy with a glass of milk!

MAKES
15 COOKIES

SERVING SIZE
1 cookie

IMMUNE-
BOOSTING
FOODS: ①

Baking sheet coated with cooking spray or lined with a silicone baking mat

1½ cups (375 mL) unbleached all-purpose flour

1 tsp (5 mL) ground cinnamon

1 tsp (5 mL) baking soda

1 tsp (5 mL) salt

¾ cup (175 mL) canola oil

¼ cup (60 mL) granulated sugar

¾ cup (175 mL) packed light brown sugar

1 large egg, beaten

1 cup (250 mL) rolled oats

1 cup (250 mL) semi-sweet chocolate chips

PREHEAT THE OVEN TO 350°F (180°C)

1 In a medium bowl, sift together the flour, cinnamon, baking soda and salt.

2 In a separate medium bowl, whisk together the oil, granulated sugar, brown sugar and egg. Add the dry ingredients to the wet ingredients and stir to combine. Do not overmix. Fold in the oats and chocolate chips until evenly distributed.

3 Scoop 3 tbsp (45 mL) of the dough and, using clean hands, roll into a ball and place on the prepared baking sheet, leaving 1 inch (2.5 cm) between cookies. Repeat with the remaining dough to make a total of 15 cookies. Using clean hands, slightly press down on each cookie.

4 Bake until a tester inserted into a cookie or two comes out clean, 14 to 16 minutes. Remove the baking sheet from the oven and transfer the cookies to a wire rack. Let cool for 10 minutes before eating.

> **TOBY'S TIPS**
>
> Try swapping the chocolate chips for raisins.
>
> To include more immune-boosting foods, swap half of the chocolate chips for chopped walnuts.

Fresh Strawberry Cupcakes
WITH STRAWBERRY GLAZE

SERVING SIZE
1 cupcake

IMMUNE-
BOOSTING
FOODS: ②

Tasting strawberries right off the plant is like eating nature's candy. These cupcakes use the red gems in the both the cake and glaze for a sweet treat bursting with the freshness of strawberries.

12-cup muffin pan coated with nonstick cooking spray

1¼ cups (300 mL) unbleached all-purpose flour

1 cup (250 mL) white whole wheat flour or 100% whole wheat flour

1 tsp (5 mL) baking powder

½ tsp (2 mL) baking soda

¼ tsp (1 mL) salt

¼ cup (60 mL) unsalted butter, melted

6 tbsp (90 mL) canola oil

¾ cup (175 mL) packed light brown sugar

1 cup (250 mL) low-fat (1%) milk

3 large eggs, beaten

1 tsp (5 mL) vanilla extract

1 cup (250 mL) thinly sliced strawberries

GLAZE

1 lb (500 g) strawberries, stems removed and thinly sliced

¾ cup (175 mL) water

⅓ cup (75 mL) granulated sugar

1 tsp (5 mL) lemon juice

½ tsp (3 mL) vanilla extract

2 tsp (10 mL) cornstarch

PREHEAT THE OVEN TO 350°F (180°C)

1 In a medium bowl, sift together the all-purpose flour, white whole wheat flour, baking powder, baking soda and salt. Gently stir to combine. Set aside.

2 In a large bowl, whisk together the butter and oil until combined. Add the brown sugar and whisk to combine. Add the milk and eggs and whisk to incorporate. Whisk in the vanilla extract.

3 Slowly add the dry ingredients to the wet ingredients, gently folding until completely combined. Add the strawberries and gently fold to combine. Scoop a heaping ¼ cup (60 mL) of the batter into each well of the muffin pan. Gently tap the pan on the counter several times to remove any air bubbles.

4 Bake until a tester inserted in the center of a cupcake comes out clean, about 25 minutes. Remove from the oven and let cool for 5 minutes in the pan before transferring to a wire rack. Cool completely.

5 FOR THE GLAZE: In a medium saucepan, add the strawberries, ½ cup (125 mL) of the water, the sugar, lemon juice and vanilla extract. Bring the mixture to a boil over high heat, stirring occasionally. Reduce the

heat to low and simmer, stirring occasionally, about 10 minutes. Using the back of a mixing spoon, break the pieces of strawberries apart. Remove the saucepan from the heat and let cool for 5 minutes.

6 Pour the strawberry mixture through a strainer and into a medium bowl. Using a wooden spoon, press as much of the juice through the strainer as possible. Discard the strawberry pulp in the strainer.

7 In a small bowl, whisk the remaining $\frac{1}{4}$ cup (60 mL) water with the cornstarch.

8 Pour the juice back into the saucepan and add the cornstarch mixture. Bring the mixture to a boil over high heat and whisk constantly until the mixture thickens, about 3 minutes. Remove the saucepan from the heat and let the glaze cool for 15 minutes.

9 Dip the top of each cooled cupcake into the glaze and then place on a plate. Repeat with the remaining cupcakes. Refrigerate the cupcakes until the glaze is set, at least 20 minutes. Serve immediately or store in a sealable container in the refrigerator for up to 3 days.

TOBY'S TIP To melt the butter, place in a microwave-safe bowl, then microwave on High for 30 to 45 seconds. Let cool for several minutes before using.

Grape Popsicles

MAKES 12

SERVING SIZE
1 popsicle

**IMMUNE-
BOOSTING
FOODS: ②**

Popsicles are a favorite dessert in my house, but as a mom and dietitian, I don't love all the sugar that tends to be added to many store-bought popsicles. That is why I opt to make my own, so I have full control over the ingredients.

Blender

12 standard popsicle molds

2 cups (500 mL) red seedless grapes

1½ cups (375 mL) nonfat vanilla Greek yogurt

1 tbsp (15 mL) pure maple syrup

Juice of 1 lemon

1 Place the grapes, yogurt, maple syrup, and lemon juice in a blender and blend on High until smooth, about 1 minute.

2 Divide the mixture evenly among the twelve standard popsicle molds. Cover and place in the freezer until frozen, at least 4 hours. Serve cold.

TOBY'S TIP | If you want to get that cool white and purple swirl in your popsicles, place the Greek yogurt in a medium bowl and set aside. Blend the grapes, maple syrup and lemon juice until smooth. Pour the grape mixture into the yogurt and gently stir until slightly incorporated then divide among the popsicle molds. You will get fewer popsicles (about eight).

Banana Walnut Cake
WITH CREAM CHEESE FROSTING

I tend to have leftover bananas, but I hate letting them go to waste! I try to find baking recipes to use them in, and this is one cake I love to make. It's a delicious way to help minimize food waste in my home and yours.

9-inch (23 cm) round cake pan coated with nonstick cooking spray

1 cup (250 mL) unbleached all-purpose flour

1 cup (250 mL) whole wheat flour or white whole wheat flour

1 tsp (5 mL) ground cinnamon

1 tsp (5 mL) baking powder

1 tsp (5 mL) baking soda

$\frac{1}{8}$ tsp (0.5 mL) salt

$\frac{1}{4}$ cup (60 mL) unsalted butter, softened

$\frac{1}{4}$ cup (60 mL) reduced-fat (2%) plain Greek yogurt

$\frac{1}{2}$ cup (125 mL) packed light brown sugar

$\frac{1}{4}$ cup (60 mL) pure maple syrup

3 bananas, mashed

2 large eggs

1 tsp (5 mL) vanilla extract

1 cup (250 mL) low-fat (1%) milk

$\frac{3}{4}$ cup (175 mL) walnuts, coarsely chopped, plus more for garnish

FROSTING

8 oz (250 mL) cream cheese

$\frac{1}{4}$ cup (60 mL) reduced-fat (2%) plain Greek yogurt

$\frac{1}{4}$ cup (60 mL) reduced-fat milk

$\frac{1}{2}$ tsp (2 mL) vanilla extract

$\frac{3}{4}$ cup (175 mL) confectioners' (icing) sugar

PREHEAT THE OVEN TO 350°F (180°C)

1 In a large bowl, sift together the all-purpose flour, whole wheat flour, cinnamon, baking powder, baking soda and salt.

2 Using an electric mixer, beat the butter and Greek yogurt on high speed until smooth. Add the brown sugar and maple syrup and continue beating until creamy. Add the bananas, eggs and vanilla and continue to beat on high until the mixture is smooth. Add half the dry ingredients into the wet ingredients and beat on low speed until incorporated. While mixing, alternate adding the milk and the remaining dry ingredients until combined. Add the walnuts and use a spoon to gently fold into the batter until evenly distributed. Do not overmix.

3 Pour the batter into the prepared cake pan and transfer to the center rack of the oven. Bake until a toothpick inserted into the center of the cake comes out clean, 25 to 30 minutes. Turn the cake out onto a wire rack and set aside for at least 15 minutes to cool.

4 TO MAKE THE FROSTING: In a large bowl, add the cream cheese, yogurt, milk and vanilla. Using an electric mixer, beat until creamy. Add the confectioners' sugar, 1 to 2 tbsp (15 to 30 mL) at a time. Continue mixing on high speed until incorporated.

5 Using a spatula, spread the frosting evenly over the top of the cake. Sprinkle with extra walnuts and serve immediately.

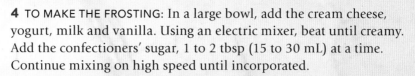

TOBY'S TIP | To reduce the fat of the frosting, use reduced-fat cream cheese or Neufchatel cheese.

Grilled Pears
WITH WHIPPED YOGURT CREAM

Grilled fruit is a mouthwatering way to enjoy fruit. Pair it with a tasty immune-boosting Greek yogurt cream sauce and you've got a winning dessert every time!

SERVING SIZE
$^1/_2$ pear plus
$^1/_3$ cup (75 mL)
cream

IMMUNE-
BOOSTING
FOODS: ③

Grill pan coated with nonstick cooking spray or a grill brushed with canola oil

PEARS

2 tbsp (30 mL) canola oil

1 tsp (5 mL) ground cinnamon

$^1/_8$ tsp (0.5 mL) ground nutmeg

2 pears, halved lengthwise and cored

CREAM

1 cup (250 mL) nonfat vanilla Greek yogurt

$^1/_4$ cup (60 mL) heavy or whipping (35%) cream

1 tbsp (15 mL) pure maple syrup

TO SERVE

$^1/_4$ cup (60 mL) unsalted dry roasted almonds, coarsely chopped

1 TO MAKE THE PEARS: Place the grill pan over medium heat or heat the grill to medium.

2 In a medium bowl, whisk the oil, cinnamon and nutmeg. Add the pears and toss to evenly coat.

3 Transfer the pears to the prepared grill pan or grill and cook without moving until slightly browned, about 5 minutes, turning them once halfway through.

4 TO MAKE THE CREAM: In a large bowl, add the Greek yogurt, cream and maple syrup. Using an electric mixer fitted with a whisk attachment, beat on low speed until the Greek yogurt and cream are incorporated. Increase the speed to high and continue whipping until soft peaks form, about 3 minutes.

5 TO SERVE: Place a pear half in each of four dessert bowls and top with $^1/_3$ cup (75 mL) of the whipped yogurt cream. Sprinkle each bowl with 1 tbsp (15 mL) of the almonds. Serve immediately.

TOBY'S TIP | Swap the pears for apples.

Immune-Boosting Brownies

My three teenage kids are my taste testers for many of my recipes. So how did these brownies fare in the "kid test"? Let's just say, there were only crumbs left in the morning.

SERVING SIZE
1 piece

IMMUNE-BOOSTING FOODS: ②

Blender

8-inch by 8-inch (20 cm) glass baking dish coated with nonstick cooking spray

7 oz (210 g) semi-sweet chocolate chips, divided

1/4 cup (60 mL) unsalted butter, cut into several pieces

1 can (14 to 19 oz/398 to 540 mL) low-sodium chickpeas, drained and rinsed

1/4 cup (60 mL) canola oil

3/4 cup (175 mL) unbleached all-purpose flour

1/2 cup (125 mL) unsweetened cocoa powder

1 tsp (5 mL) baking powder

1/2 tsp (1 mL) kosher salt

1/2 cup (125 mL) pure maple syrup

1/2 cup (125 mL) nonfat milk

2 large eggs, beaten

1 tsp (5 mL) vanilla extract

1/2 cup (125 mL) unsalted dry roasted walnuts, coarsely chopped

PREHEAT THE OVEN TO 350°F (180°C)

1 In a small microwave-safe bowl, add 4 oz (125 g) of the chocolate chips and the butter. Microwave on High for 30 seconds, stirring, then microwave for another 30 seconds, until melted. Set the bowl aside and let cool slightly.

2 Place the chickpeas and canola oil in the blender and purée until smooth.

3 In a medium bowl, sift together the flour, cocoa powder, baking powder and salt.

4 In a separate medium bowl, whisk together the maple syrup, milk, eggs and vanilla extract until incorporated. Slowly add in the chocolate mixture, whisking until completely combined. Add the chickpea mixture, whisking until completely combined.

5 Add the dry ingredients to the wet ingredients and gently fold until combined. Fold in the remaining 3 oz (90 g) chocolate chips and the walnuts until incorporated.

6 Pour the batter into the prepared baking dish and use a spatula to even out the top. Gently tap the dish on the counter several times to remove any air bubbles. Bake until a tester inserted into the center of the pan comes out clean, 55 to 60 minutes. Remove the baking dish from the oven and let cool for about 10 minutes.

7 Cut into 2-inch by 2-inch (5 cm by 5 cm) pieces. Serve warm or store covered in the baking dish or in a sealable container at room temperature for up to 5 days.

> **TOBY'S TIP** | Swap the semi-sweet chocolate for 60% bittersweet (dark) chocolate or milk chocolate.

Acknowledgments

There are many people I want to thank for making this cookbook possible. My children, Schoen, Ellena and Micah, thank you for taste-test approving every recipe in this cookbook. All three of you have always been supportive of my career and I love you very much. Micah, thank you for taking the time during your COVID virtual school to help me test recipes. Thank you to all my children for making cooking nightly dinners easier by pitching in to cook meals as a family.

A big thank-you to Katy Zanville, MS, RDN, LDN, for being the best assistant and helping me test some of the recipes in this cookbook. Thank you to my dietetic internship intern Dominika Tomczyk, who quickly learned how to test recipes and did a fabulous job helping on this project.

Thank you to my literary agent Sally Ekus from The Lisa Ekus Group for your support and kindness. Many thanks to Robert Dees and Meredith Dees from Robert Rose Inc. for teaming up with me on this project and believing in me. To my editor, Kate Bolen, thank you for your continued support and guidance throughout this project. I cannot think of a better editor to work with than you! I love your constant attention and love for each and every project we work on together. Thanks to Kevin Cockburn for the design of this book. Lastly, thank you to Ashley Lima for taking the most amazing photos of the recipes in this book.

Index